TAX POLICY
AND THE ECONOMY 4

edited by ***Lawrence H. Summers***

National Bureau of Economic Research
The MIT Press, Cambridge, Massachusetts

Send orders and business correspondence to:
The MIT Press
55 Hayward Street
Cambridge, MA 02142

In the United Kingdom, continental Europe, and the Middle East and Africa, send orders and business correspondence to:
The MIT Press Ltd.
126 Buckingham Palace Road
London SW1W 9SA England

ISSN: 0892-8649
ISBN: hardcover 0-262-19296-9
      paperback 0-262-69140-X

Library of Congress number 87-644377

CONTENTS

INTRODUCTION

Lawrence H. Summers
Harvard University and NBER

While the 1986 Tax Reform Act was as sweeping as any in the history of the American income tax, it did not put an end to discussions of tax reform. The combined pressure of continuing budget deficits and increasing concern about the ability of the United States to compete in an increasingly open world economy has led to continuing discussion of further tax reforms. Tax policy debates continue to occupy the attention of public officials, the business community, tax attorneys, and the general public. Capital gains tax reform was one of the most contentious issues considered by the Congress in 1989, and is likely to be debated further in the near future.

Economic research can make an important contribution to tax policy debates by providing quantitative information on both the distribution of the burdens associated with various tax changes, and on the likely effects of various proposals on economic efficiency. Tax changes are often credited or blamed for a host of changes in the American economy ranging from increases in corporate leverage to declines in personal saving. Economic research makes an important indirect contribution to tax policy when it evaluates the veracity of these claims.

This volume, like its three predecessors, collects a number of economic studies of issues of immediate relevance to ongoing studies of tax reform. Each of the studies is at the forefront of modern work in public economics. But the conclusions are presented in a way that is intended to be accessible to non-economists who are concerned with the development of tax policy. In the remainder of this introduction, I shall summarize the five papers included in the present volume.

Daniel Feenberg's and my paper, "Who Benefits from Capital Gains Tax Reductions?" examines the distribution of capital gains benefits along several dimensions. Examining the distribution of benefits across income classes, we find that, contrary to some recent claims, the lion's share of the benefits of any capital gains reductions go to high income taxpayers. By a variety of measures, the richest 2 percent of Americans receive more than 50 percent of all capital gains. Capital gains on corporate stocks are even more concentrated among high income taxpayers. Because moderate income taxpayers typically hold their assets longer, and enjoy smaller capital gains than their higher income counterparts, it turns out that indexing the basis of capital assets is considerably more progressive than reducing capital gains tax rates.

Because some assets such as new equipment may yield more external benefits than others and because the current tax system probably favors some types of investments, it is of interest to know what types of assets would benefit from a capital gains tax reduction. Feenberg and I find for a variety of capital gains tax reduction options that less than half of the benefits go to corporate assets, and that in most cases real estate is the principal beneficiary of capital gains tax reductions. This bias is especially strong in the case of indexation proposals. We also find that most capital gains are realized on assets that have been held for 10 or more years. This implies that over a five year period, close to 80 percent of the benefits of capital gains tax reductions are likely to accrue to assets that were already in place when the tax cut was enacted. Since relatively few short-term capital gains are realized, it is unlikely that graduating tax rates by holding period for taxable investors would have much impact on the turnover of financial assets.

The paper "Treatment of Capital Income in Recent Tax Reforms and the Cost of Capital in Industrialized Countries" by Eytan Sheshinski contrasts the 1986 U.S. Tax Reform Act with recent reforms in other countries. While top marginal tax rates have fallen sharply and the tax base has been broadened almost everywhere, Sheshinski finds no similar uniformity in the treatment of capital income. The United States is alone in having embraced the concept of uniformity in the taxation of capital income. In most other countries, interest, capital gains, and to a lesser extent dividends continue to be heavily tax favored. Traditionally, other countries have been less generous than the United States in permitting individuals to deduct interest in computing their taxes, but the gap has narrowed with the U.S. decision to phase out consumer interest deductions.

Mark Gertler and R. Glenn Hubbard's paper "Taxation, Corporate Capital Structure, and Financial Distress" offers some reflections on the role of taxation in corporate leverage decisions. During the 1980s, corporate leverage has increased sharply. In the last year or so, a number of highly leveraged firms have encountered severe financial distress, leading some observers to worry that current tax rules endanger financial stability. Gertler and Hubbard review recent developments in economic theory which highlight the potential benefits and costs of debt finance. They argue that firms would choose optimal capital structures, trading off the benefits and costs of debt finance, if there were no tax bias in favor of debt. They then argue that present tax rules induce firms to accept more risk of cyclical distress and so endanger financial stability. Gertler and Hubbard conclude their paper by suggesting a number of reforms that have the potential to reduce the tax bias in favor of debt finance.

Alan Auerbach and Laurence Kotlikoff's paper "Demographics, Fiscal Policy, and U.S. Saving in the 1980s and Beyond" explores the implications of demographic changes for U.S. saving behavior. Given the large changes in the age structure of the U.S. population that are likely over the next 40 years, this topic is of considerable importance for budget policy generally and Social Security policy in particular. Auerbach and Kotlikoff use data on the savings of persons in different age groups in an effort to forecast the likely effects of demographic change on the American saving rate. They find that for about the next 30 years, demographic factors are likely to push the American saving rate upward. They suggest that this may lead the U.S. current account to move into surplus by the year 2000.

Auerbach and Kotlikoff observe that demographic factors cannot account for the decline in personal and private saving during the 1980s. They therefore examine a number of other factors, including the strong stock market, increased consumer borrowing, and reductions in the precautionary demand for saving. In the end, however, they are unable to fully resolve the question of why saving declined in the 1980s. They suggest that the decline in saving during the 1970s reflects non-demographic factors and so does not call into question their conclusion that demographic factors will push the American saving rate upward in the years to come.

Lawrence Goulder's paper "Implications of Introducing U.S. Withholding Taxes on Foreigners' Interest Income" addresses an issue that has attracted increasing attention as the magnitude of foreign investment in the U.S. has increased during the 1980s. Using a computable general equilibrium model of the U.S. as an open economy that he developed in an earlier work, Goulder concludes that the introduction of a statutory 30 percent U.S. withholding tax on foreigners' interest income would make Americans better off if foreign governments do not retaliate. He also finds that it would reduce the American trade balance in the short run, but would exacerbate it in the long run. On the other hand, he finds that if foreigners retaliated, the introduction of a withholding tax on interest income paid to foreigners would make Americans worse off. In addition to those efficiency arguments, Goulder also considers a number of equity arguments made for and against proposals to introduce a withholding tax.

ACKNOWLEDGMENTS

I am grateful to Deborah Mankiw who has assisted in every stage of this project with good cheer and great skill. Kirsten Foss and Ilana Hardesty handled with their usual efficiency all the logistics for the conference at which these papers were presented. Martin Feldstein provided the original inspiration for the series of which this volume is a part. Finally, I am grateful to the authors of the papers included here for their hard work and skillful analysis.

Lawrence H. Summers

WHO BENEFITS FROM CAPITAL GAINS TAX REDUCTIONS?

Daniel Feenberg
NBER

Lawrence Summers
Harvard University and NBER

EXECUTIVE SUMMARY

This paper examines the distribution of the benefits associated with reductions in capital gains taxes. Plans which reduce capital gains taxes by excluding a fixed fraction of capital gains from taxable income, by taxing real rather than nominal gains, and by using a sliding scale capital gains exclusion are considered. We reach three main conclusions.

1. Using plausible measures of economic status, capital gains receipts are highly concentrated among those with high incomes. The richest 2 percent of Americans receive more than 50 percent of all capital gains. Claims that capital gains recipients only appear to be rich because their capital gains income is transitory are not supported by longitudinal data. Likewise, claims that a large fraction of the benefits from capital gains tax reductions flow to middle income taxpayers result from failing to consider tax shelters. Capital gains on corporate stocks are considerably more concentrated among high income individuals than capital gains on other assets.

2. There are important differences in the distributional consequences of different approaches to reducing capital gains taxes. Indexation yields greater benefits to lower income taxpayers than a general capital gains exclusion because they typically hold assets longer before selling them, and because they typically enjoy smaller gains than higher income taxpayers. Indexation also favors real estate over corporate stocks to a much greater extent than does a general exclusion. A sliding scale capital gains tax cut, based on the amount of time an asset is held has distributional consequences very similar to a general exclusion.

3. Most capital gains are realized on assets that were held for 10 or more years. Reductions in capital gains taxes would, for many years, benefit primarily assets that are already in place. Confining capital gains relief to future gains would substantially reduce the revenue cost of capital gains reform.

Proposals to reduce taxes on capital gains remain controversial. Disagreements stem from three sources. First, different observers with different values assess even agreed-on outcomes differently. Some regard increasing economic growth as of paramount importance, while others place more emphasis on distributional effects. Second, there are differences of opinion about the likely response of economic behavior to changes in capital gains tax rates. Proponents believe that capital gains cuts will have major effects on investment incentives and economic efficiency while opponents are skeptical of the importance of these effects and stress certain perverse incentives created by capital gains reductions. Third, there are different views about who will be the direct beneficiaries of capital gains cuts. Views differ about whether capital gains tax reductions primarily benefit high or middle income taxpayers, investors in new business or in tax shelters, and future investors or those who have invested in the past.

Disagreements over values are inherently unreconcilable. Disputes about the incentive and revenue effects of various tax reforms are potentially reconcilable, though considerable controversy remains. The question of who benefits from capital gains tax cuts is directly answerable with available longitudinal data on the returns of individual taxpayers. This paper uses these data to examine the distribution of the benefits from four different capital gains reform proposals: an across the board tax cut on long-term assets similar to the one proposed by the Bush administration; indexation of the basis on capital assets; a sliding scale capital gains tax rate that declines with the length of time for which an asset is held; and an alternative like the one considered by the Senate in the fall of 1989 that offered taxpayers a choice between indexing gains and length-of-time-based exclusion. We focus on three aspects of the distribution of the benefits from capital gains tax cuts.

First, *will the benefits of capital gains tax cuts flow primarily to very wealthy taxpayers or will they be relatively evenly distributed?* Income in a single year inclusive of capital gains may be a very poor indicator of a household's economic status. We therefore explore the distribution of capital gains tax liabilities by a variety of measures of economic well being, including average income over a four-year period, an estimate of taxable wealth, and for those who have not yet retired, wage and salary income. *Regardless of what measure of economic status we use, we find that the majority of capital gains tax preferences go to those in the top 0.5 to 2 percent of the income distribution.* Analyses suggesting otherwise are flawed by elementary errors such as using current wage and salary income to measure the economic position of those who have retired, or failing to take full account of preference income in assessing taxpayers' affluence.

While any reduction in capital gains tax burdens primarily benefits high income households, there are important differences in the distributional consequences of different plans. Because very high income taxpayers have typically earned larger capital gains, relative to the price at which they bought their assets, they gain less from indexing schemes which raise the basis on the sale of assets than do taxpayers who are less well off. For example, we estimate that 43 percent of an across the board exclusion for capital gains would go to the taxpayers with less than $100,000 in AGI whereas 62 percent of the benefits of indexing capital gains would go to the same group. The distributional consequences of the pure sliding scale plan are quite similar to those of an across the board capital gains exclusion.

Second, *which types of investment will benefit from capital gains tax reform?* Many observers concerned with the competitiveness of American industry regard spurring investment in new equipment or technology as a higher priority than spurring investment in real estate or short-term financial instruments. Others are concerned with the distribution of benefits across different types of assets because they believe that the tax code already discriminates against certain classes of investment and believe that redress is appropriate. For the four capital gains reform proposals we consider, we estimate the fraction of relief going to different asset categories.

Our results suggest that, in general, *less than half of the benefits of capital gains tax cuts go to owners of corporate stock.* Only a small fraction of the benefits go to venture capital or small businesses. Nearly half of the reported capital gains involve real estate. There are some interesting differences between the effects of different capital gains cut reductions. For example, 27 percent of the benefit of inflation indexing goes to owners of corporate stock and 56 percent to owners of land and real estate. On the other hand, an across the board capital gains exclusion favors stockholders (42 percent of the benefit) at the expense of real estate investors (35 percent). The other plans we consider have intermediate effects.

Third, *to what extent will capital gains tax cuts benefit capital that is already in place?* For each of our four plans, we estimate the fraction of the benefits conferred in the five years following reform that will go to investments that had already been made at the time a plan was put into effect. We find that for each of the plans considered *between 75 and 80 percent of first five years' tax relief will be a windfall to assets that are already in place.* The windfall fraction is greater for the exclusion plans and less for indexing. If, as proponents suggest, capital gains tax reductions would spur realizations, the fraction of windfall gains would be even higher. These results imply that very substantial reductions in the budgetary cost of capital gains tax reductions could be achieved by making them prospective.

The remainder of the paper is organized as follows. Section I considers the effects of capital gains tax cuts on the distribution of income. Section II examines their effects on different assets. Section III considers the distribution of benefits between past and future investments. Section IV examines how taking account of incentive effects might modify the conclusions of the earlier analysis and offers some concluding observations.

I. CAPITAL GAINS TAX CUTS AND THE DISTRIBUTION OF INCOME

This section examines the effects of capital gains tax reforms on taxpayers with differing incomes. As a number of analysts have pointed out, there are reasons for doubting that simple tabulations of who pays capital gains tax payments by income class say very much about the economic well-being of those who benefit from capital gains relief. First, when individuals sell assets on which they have large accrued gains, their single year income overstates the standard of living that they can sustain. Second, for taxpayers who successfully shelter income, adjusted gross income may understate true standards of living. The same is true of efforts to use wage and salary income to proxy economic well-being when retired people are included in the sample. In order to ad-

TABLE 1
Distribution of Capital Gains Realization by AGI

Percentile rank	AGI breakpoint	Cumulative percent of AGI	Cumulative percent of gains*
.5	203.0	8.0	54.0
1.0	145.0	11.0	61.0
2.0	106.0	15.0	68.0
5.0	75.6	24.0	75.0
10.0	59.0	35.0	80.0
20.0	44.1	50.0	84.0
50.0	20.8	85.0	91.0
100.0		100.0	100.0

Source: 1986 Tax Model and authors' calculations. Dollar amounts in thousands of 1989 dollars.

* Schedule D and non-schedule D net gains before capital gains deduction. Losses limited to $3,000.

dress these issues, we examine the distribution of realized capital gains by a number of different measures of economic status.

Table 1 presents the distribution of capital gains income by taxpayers' adjusted gross income. The data are drawn from NBER 1986 Individual Income Tax Model. They reveal that capital gains are much more concentrated than most other forms of income. Persons in the top 0.5 percent of the income distribution receive 54 percent of all capital gains compared with 8 percent of total income. It appears that the top 2 percent of the population receives almost eight times as much capital gains income as the bottom 50 percent of the population. If adjusted gross income is accepted as a satisfactory measure of real affluence, it is hard to escape the conclusion that the proximate benefits of capital gains tax reductions are rich taxpayers.

It is often argued that statistics like those in Table 1 are very misleading because a sizable fraction of capital gains go to people of modest means who sell their home or their business and have their income artificially inflated for a single year. In order to examine this issue, Table 2 makes use of the most recently available panel data on individual tax returns. The data cover the period from 1979 to 1984. Besides the differences in time period, the panel data are not comparable to the information in Table 1 because the panel sample contains relatively few high income taxpayers.[1] Nonetheless, the panel information can be used to

---

[1] The standard tax file is a stratified random sample with weights attached to each return. The panel sample is a purely random sample of tax returns.

TABLE 2
Distribution of Capital Gains Realizations by Average and
Annual Income

| Percentile rank | Annual AGI | | Average AGI* | |
| | With net capital gains | | With net capital gains | |
	Income breakpoint	Cumulative net gain	Income breakpoint	Cumulative gains
.5	217.0	42.2	211.0	36.1
1.0	152.0	50.3	144.0	42.3
2.0	115.0	56.5	110.0	49.4
5.0	82.5	66.7	80.7	59.2
10.0	65.7	72.4	63.8	65.9
20.0	50.5	78.7	49.6	74.4
50.0	37.5	89.1	26.6	87.7
100.0		100.0		100.0

* *Source:* 1979–1984 Panel File and authors' calculations. All dollar amounts in 1989 dollars. Sample is pooled 1979–1984 tax returns for taxpayers with four or more returns represented.

get an indication of the importance of the distortion caused by looking at only a single year's income.

The results in Table 2 on the distribution of capital gains income by total AGI inclusive of capital gains suggest that reliance on a single year's income in assessing the distributional impact of capital gains changes does not greatly distort the picture. For the panel sample, the data suggest that when income in a single year is studied, 50 percent of capital gains go to the top 1 percent of income recipients, whereas when average income is used, 43 percent of capital gains go the top 1 percent of income recipients. Similarly, using four-year average data reduces the share of capital gains going to the top 5 percent of capital gains recipients from 67 to 59 percent. To put these figures in perspective, note that the share of all income going to the top 1 percent of the population on an annual basis is 9 percent but falls to 8 percent on a four-year average basis. This suggests that capital gains income is not more transitory than most other components of income.

This inference is supported by the recent analysis of capital gains recipients by Slemrod et al. They report that half of the capital gains in the years 1981–1984 are realized by taxpayers with gains reported in each of the four years, and that only 6–13 percent of the gains (depending on the year selected) are reported by taxpayers realizing capital gains in only one of the four years. While they find that using average income over a several-year period considerably reduces the share of capital gains received by the $200,000 and over income category, this is in a sense a statistical artifact. It occurs primarily because taking average income over a four-year period reduces the fraction of taxpayers in the $200,000 and above category.

An alternative way of examining the distribution of the benefits from capital gains tax cuts, is to look at the distribution of capital gains by income categories that exclude capital gains. Two approaches are suggested in this regard. Sometimes, the distribution of capital gains by income class exclusive of capital gains is examined. Alternatively, it is suggested that wage and salary income is a preferable proxy for true economic income. Both of these approaches are problematic since there is no reason why capital gains are not as much income as interest receipts or dividend payments. Furthermore, as we have just demonstrated, most capital gains do not represent transitory income. However, because statistics on the non-capital gains income of capital gains recipients are often used to support the claim that a substantial fraction of capital gains relief beneficiaries would be middle class, it is worth examining further the economic position of capital gains beneficiaries.

The first column of Table 3 reports the distribution of capital gains beneficiaries by non-capital gains income. When capital gains income is excluded, the distribution of capital gains appears to be much more egalitarian. The top 0.5 percent of recipients of non-capital gains income receive only 24 percent of all capital gains. Furthermore, the share of capital gains going to the half of the population with lower incomes rises to 11 percent when capital gains income is included in income, and to 30 percent when it is excluded. Statistics of this type have been used by the Wall Street Journal's editors and others to illustrate that the middle class is an important potential beneficiary of cuts in capital gains taxes.

Before accepting this conclusion, it is worthwhile to consider other characteristics of "low or moderate income" taxpayers who receive substantial capital gains income. Toward this end, the second column of Table 3 looks at the distribution of capital gains by income where income is expanded to include only positive items. This excludes tax shelter losses. It turns out to have a major impact on the distributional consequences of reductions in capital gains taxes. The share of capital gains received by the 0.5 percent of the population rises from 24 to 41 percent, and the share received by the lower half falls from 30 to 11 percent.

The striking differences between the tabulations which include and exclude loss items in measuring income suggest that there may be large differences between middle income families with and without capital gains receipts. Table 4 compares this group to other taxpayers with

TABLE 3
Distributions of Capital Gains Realizations by Other Income Measures

Percentile rank	AGI less capital gains		Positive income items*		Wages and salaries**		Taxable wealth imputation***	
	Breakpoints	Cumulative capital gains	Breakpoints	Cumulative capital gains	Breakpoints	Cumulative capital gains	Breakpoints	Cumulative capital gains
0.5	173.0	24.0	213.0	41.0	159.0	37.0	876.0	41.0
1.0	128.0	28.0	151.0	48.0	121.0	47.0	569.0	49.0
2.0	98.8	33.0	112.0	55.0	97.1	56.0	365.0	57.0
5.0	72.9	39.0	80.4	64.0	74.0	66.0	173.0	70.0
10.0	57.6	44.0	62.1	70.0	59.2	74.0	85.1	80.0
20.0	43.2	49.0	45.7	77.0	44.9	83.0	25.3	89.0
50.0	20.3	59.0	21.3	90.0	21.8	93.0	.94	98.0
100.0		100.0		100.0		100.0		100.0

Sources: 1986 Tax Model File and authors' calculations. Dollar amounts in thousands of 1989 dollars.

* Sum of positive components of AGI, except capital gains realizations.

** Sample for this column limited to returns with wages and salaries greater than $5,000 and greater than 90 percent of positive income items (defined above).

*** Sum of interest income capitalized at .0971 and dividends capitalized at .0364.

TABLE 4
Shelters and Capital Gains Income

	Weighted mean shelters*	
AGI	No capital gains	With capital gains
0	34,100	581,400
12,000	311	27,400
25,000	578	16,700
50,000	942	14,700
100,000	2,270	25,100
200,000	11,500	28,900
500,000	45,800	79,700
and up	187,000	639,000

Source: 1986 Tax Model File and authors' calculations. Dollar amounts in thousands of 1989 dollars. Potential negative items include Schedule C, Farm, Estate and Trust, Rent and Royalties. Small Business Corporations, Capital losses (Schedule D or 4797) and "other income." Sample restricted to returns with net gains.

* Equally weighted for returns with no capital gains. Other returns weighted by capital gains realized.

similar incomes but no capital gains. Clear differences emerge. Whereas the average taxpayer with an income between $12,000 and $25,000 reported only $578 in losses, the average dollar of capital gains accruing to a person in this income class was associated with $16,700 in reported losses. It turns out that fully 25 percent of capital gains are received by taxpayers whose non-capital gains income is negative. While it is difficult with the available information to pinpoint precisely the source of the tax losses that often coincide with capital gains income, it seems reasonable to suspect that tax shelter activity plays an important role.

Almost certainly, the true economic position of someone with a $75,000 income after reporting a tax loss of $50,000 is more favorable than someone with the same income and no negative tax items. Claims that a large fraction of capital gains are received by persons with moderate income should be accompanied by the further observation that most moderate-income recipients of capital gains had moderate incomes only because they were able to report tax losses.

These inferences are supported by a 1989 CBO staff memorandum that examined the distribution of capital gains income by a measure of expanded AGI. This measure includes items like tax-exempt interest and adds back an estimate of tax shelter losses. The CBO reports that 57.6 percent of gains went to the 0.5 percent of all taxpayers with income greater than $200,000 in 1985. Even when capital gains are entirely excluded from income, it appears that nearly 40 percent of capital gains go to taxpayers with among the top 0.5 percent of expanded income.

The third column of Table 3 examines the distribution of capital gains by wage and salary income—another set of statistics that has been used to suggest that the middle class benefits substantially from cuts in capital gains taxes. Wage and salary income is misleading as an indicator of economic status because taxpayers who have retired and so no longer have wage and salary income appear poor even though they may in fact be quite wealthy. The same is true of the owners of small businesses. In order to address these issues, we include in our tabulation only taxpayers for whom wage and salary income represents more than 90 percent of non-capital gains positive income. The results indicate that once taxpayers who derive substantial income from sources other than wages and salaries and capital gains are excluded, the distribution of capital gains income again appears to be highly skewed toward the rich. Nearly 56 percent of capital gains go the highest-income 2 percent of taxpayers, who are primarily dependent on wages and salaries.

As an alternative approach to assessing the economic well-being of capital gains beneficiaries, the last column of Table 3 reports the distribution of capital gains by "taxable wealth." We estimate taxable wealth by grossing up dividends by the average yield on the stock market and interest payments by the average short-term interest rate. The results, in line with our other tabulations, suggest that more than half of capital gains go to the wealthiest 2 percent of the population.

The evidence in Tables 1–4 suggests that the standard tabulation of capital gains income by AGI overstates slightly the concentration of capital gains income in the upper end of the income distribution by failing to recognize that capital gains income is transitory. Of at least equal importance, the concentration of capital gains income is understated because many apparently moderate income capital gains recipients have probably reduced their reported income significantly by using tax shelters. *There is no clear-cut direction of bias in simple tabulations of the distribution of capital gains by AGI. The conclusion that most capital gains go to very high income taxpayers is robust to plausible variations in the exact income concept used to assess the issue.*

Alternative Approaches to Reducing Capital Gains Taxes

It appears that most capital gains go to those in the upper part of the distribution of true income. However, it is of some interest to examine whether or not different capital gains reduction plans have different distributional impacts. Differences might arise if, for example, the typical ratio of sale price to basis was different for taxpayers in different income categories, or if taxpayers in different income categories differed in how rapidly they turned their assets over.

We consider four plans in our analysis. The first *straight exclusion* plan is similar to the one proposed by the president during the 1988 campaign. It would exclude 40 percent of all long-term (over one year) capital gains from income, regardless of how long an asset had been held. The second, an *indexing* plan, would tax only the real component of capital gains. In order to measure the real component of gains, the purchase price of an asset is stepped up by the increase in the general price level since it was purchased before calculating the gain. Most indexation proposals and the one considered here does not allow indexing to create capital losses. The third, a *sliding scale plan*, calls for an exclusion which increases as the length of time an asset has been held rises. The plan considered here is an exclusion that increases at 5 percent a year for seven years and then reaches a maximum of 35 percent on assets sold after seven or more years. The fourth, a *combination* plan, allows taxpayers to compute their tax liability on the basis of either the indexing or the sliding scale plan and use whichever plan is more favorable.

In order to examine these plans, it is necessary to have data on the purchase date, purchase price, and sale price of individual assets along with individual returns. Without this information, it is not possible to simulate the effects of indexing or introducing a sliding scale based on holding periods. Such data exist for 1973, 1981, and 1985, having been collected by the Treasury at a cost that exceeds $1 million for each survey. Unfortunately, the Treasury has been and remains unwilling to release the 1981 and 1985 information to outside researchers. As a consequence, we have to work with 1973 information.

This creates a variety of problems. Most obviously, there is the likelihood that patterns of capital gains realization have changed over time. There is also the fact that the inflation history has certainly changed since 1973. Since inflation rates were much lower prior to 1973 than they have been over the last 15 years, there is no reason to suppose that the fraction of gains that represents real income has remained constant. In order to address this issue, we have put the data on a contemporary basis using the following procedure.

We made a strict application of Fisher's law to adjust the basis of each asset sold in 1973. That is, we assumed that inflation adjusts the nominal, but not the real, return on assets. This assumption is questionable in the presence of taxes but provides a concrete basis for analysis. The imputation inflates the sale price of assets sold in 1973 to 1992 dollars (5 percent inflation is assumed for 1989–1992), but adjusts the basis to maintain the same real rate of return over the holding period ending in 1992 as was actually earned for the holding period ending in 1973. The effect of this procedure is to keep the distribution of real capital gains income constant but to alter the magnitude of reported nominal gains on individual tax returns.

Table 5 reports the distributional consequences of the different plans. The results suggest a clear difference between indexation and other means of reducing capital gains taxes. The distribution of the benefits from each of the plans is highly skewed toward high income taxpayers. In the case of a straight exclusion of capital gains, 57 percent of the benefits would go to the 2.5 percent of taxpayers with incomes over $100,000. Relative to other plans, the distribution of the benefits from indexation is highly progressive. While taxpayers with AGI less than $75,000 (in 1990 dollars) would get 52 percent of the benefits from indexing, taxpayers in the same range would get only 34 percent of the benefits of a straight exclusion. The distributional consequences of the combination plan appear to be more like those of indexing than those of moving to a sliding scale. This is because the indexing option is more generous than the partial exclusion option for most taxpayers.

Table 6 illustrates the reason why indexation is more progressive than the other reforms considered. It reveals that the average ratio of sale price to purchase price is 65 percent for taxpayers with incomes under $75,000, but 54 percent for taxpayers with incomes over $75,000. This is in spite of the fact that holding periods were slightly greater (5.7 years vs. 4.8 years) for lower income taxpayers. Both the fact that basis starts out higher for lower income taxpayers, and their slightly longer holding periods operate to make indexation disproportionately advantageous for them. These results are consistent with the finding of Feldstein and Yitzhaki (1984) that high income taxpayers tend to earn higher returns on their investments than low income taxpayers although some kind of sampling bias might be an alternative explanation.

In assessing the result that indexation is more progressive than other methods of reducing capital gains tax burdens, it is important to recall that even its benefits are quite regressively distributed. More than half of the benefits would go to the taxpayers with incomes over $100,000.

Market Responses to Reforms

In keeping with most previous investigations of the issue, the incidence calculations presented here take no account of tax induced changes in behavior and in market conditions that might follow capital gains tax reforms. This is unavoidable given the available data, but it raises a number of questions about how the conclusion reached here that capital gains tax cuts would be regressive would be modified if behavioral effects were recognized.

First, to the extent that capital gains tax cuts led to increased capital

TABLE 5
Distribution of Benefits for Four Plans for Capital Gains Relief, By AGI Class

AGI breakpoint	Cumulative percentage of returns	Cumulative percentage of net gains	Cumulative percentage of benefit			
			Straight exclusion	Indexing	Sliding scale	Combination
0	.6	3.1	.63	.47	.57	.55
2,500	6.0	3.2	.65	.52	.59	.58
6,000	15.0	4.3	.81	.78	.72	.77
12,000	29.0	6.2	2.1	3.4	2.0	2.7
20,000	45.0	9.8	5.0	8.6	4.3	6.2
25,000	54.0	11.6	6.9	12.5	6.2	9.0
30,000	62.0	14.2	9.3	17.0	8.4	12.5
40,000	76.0	21.4	15.8	25.0	15.5	19.8
50,000	84.0	26.9	21.9	36.3	22.1	28.2
75,000	96.0	37.9	33.8	52.2	33.7	41.2
100,000	97.5	47.2	43.3	61.6	42.7	50.2
200,000	99.4	64.9	63.6	80.0	63.0	69.2
500,000	99.9	81.4	80.0	92.4	78.9	83.6
1,000,000	99.99	89.1	87.6	95.9	86.6	89.8
and up	100.0	100.0	100.0	100.0	100.0	

Source: 1973 Sales of Capital Assets, 1986 Tax Model File, and authors' calculations. Dollar amounts in 1989 dollars. Applies 1989 tax rates and recent inflation history to the 1973 distribution of asset realizations. Schedule D gains only for taxpayers with net gains.

TABLE 6
*Average Basis to Sale Price and Holding Period For Taxpayers in
Different Income Classes*

AGI	Basis/ Sale ratio	Holding period
Less than $75,000	.65	5.7 years
$75,000 or more	.54	4.8 years

Source: 1973 Sales of Capital Assets and authors' calculations. Presumes recent inflation experience (see text). Capital loss returns excluded. Schedule D sales only.

gains tax realizations, reductions in tax revenues caused by lower rates would be at least partially offset by the greater volume of realizations. This argument is relevant for the purpose of estimating the government revenue consequences of capital gains cuts, but not for addressing their distributional consequences. By assuming no behavioral changes, the calculations above *understate* the true gain to capital gains recipients associated with capital gains tax cuts. Taking account of changes in behavior would only increase the apparent advantage conferred on capital gains recipients.

Second, it is possible that capital gains cuts would lead to increases in asset values. These changes are relevant to a full assessment of the distributional consequences of capital gains tax changes. In all likelihood they are highly tilted to the upper part of the income distribution. A Federal Reserve Study (1986) has estimated that the families in the top 0.5 percent of the income distribution own 43 percent of all stock, and that families in the top 10 percent of the income distribution own 85 percent of all stock.

The evidence in this section suggests that the benefits of reductions in capital gains taxes would flow primarily to persons with high standards of living. This conclusion does not depend on just how capital gains tax relief is provided, or on what measure of income is used in the analysis as long as elementary errors are avoided. Of course, the income distribution implications of capital gains tax cuts are only one relevant aspect. In the next section, we ask what types of investment would benefit most from capital gains tax reductions.

II. WHICH TYPES OF INVESTMENT BENEFIT FROM CAPITAL GAINS TAX REDUCTIONS?

This section examines the effects of capital gains tax reductions on the holders of different types of assets. This is relevant to an assessment of

TABLE 7
Distribution of Benefits by Asset Type

	Indexing	Straight exclusion	Sliding scale	Combination
Real Estate	55.7	38.9	41.2	47.8
Stocks	27.3	42.0	39.9	33.7
Timber	.6	.7	.8	.7
Other	16.4	18.4	18.1	17.8

Source: 1973 Sales of Capital Assets, 1986 Tax Model and authors' calculations. Applies 1989 tax rates and recent inflation experience to the 1973 distribution of asset realizations. Schedule D gains only, and only for taxpayers with net gains.

the desirability of capital gains tax cuts for at least two reasons. First, it may be that there is a stronger case for spurring some types of investment than others. It is often argued, for example, that corporate investments, particularly in new plant and equipment yield external benefits to other firms. Some observers argue that offering assistance to industries engaged in international competition should be an especially high priority. Second, it is often alleged that certain types of investment (e.g., real estate) are already heavily tax-favored because they can more easily hold tax-favored debt. See, for example, Gordon Hines and Summers (1987) and Summers (1987) for a discussion of these issues. Reductions in capital gains taxes on assets that are financed by issuing debt may be seen as less desirable than reductions in taxes on other assets. Japan and a number of other nations tax capital gains on corporate stocks at a lower rate than capital gains on real estate and other assets. (See Shoven, 1989.)

Table 7 presents evidence on the fraction of the benefits of each of four capital gains reductions plans that would flow to the holders of corporate stocks, real estate investors, timber investors, and other assets. Regardless of which plan is considered, a minority of the benefits go to the holders of corporate stock. It is striking that, despite the attention it receives in discussions of the capital gains issue only a very small fraction of capital gains benefits go to timber.[2] Poterba (1989), who also considers the distribution of capital gains benefits across assets, finds notes that the share of the benefits which go to venture capital is very small. Most of the benefits go to real estate investments of various kinds and to assets that fall in the "other" category. This category includes

[2] This conclusion may be misleading because we are only examining capital gains that appear on individual Schedule D returns. This excludes depreciable business property and owner-occupied housing.

collectibles, oil and gas, and bonds, among others. Probably some capital gains from the sale of small unincorporated businesses also show up in the "other" category.

Alternative capital gains reduction plans differ considerably in their impact on different assets. While real estate investment would gain twice as much from indexing as stock market investments, stocks would actually gain more from a straight exclusion than would real estate investments. The sliding scale plan is like the straight exclusion plan but is slightly more favorable to real estate. The differences here reflect the fact that real estate investments are typically held somewhat longer than other investments and the fact that capital gains on real estate sales are typically somewhat smaller than capital gains on sales of stocks. There is considerable evidence (for example, see Summers, 1981), that increases in inflation raise real estate prices relative to stock prices. To the extent that this is the case, the conclusion reached here would be reinforced.

The finding that indexing disproportionately benefits real estate investment raises questions about the extent to which it increases neutrality, since real estate investments are more highly leveraged than other forms of investment. Increases in inflation, assuming the validity of the Fisher's law assumption maintained here, raise nominal interest rates and the value of nominal interest deductions. Because interest deductions, unlike capital gains are not deferred, the extra interest deductions on real estate investments may well exceed the increased capital gains taxes. In this case, indexing only capital gains would reduce rather than increase tax neutrality. There is also the further point that, as Gordon, Hines, and Summers (1987) document, inflation encourages tax arbitrage between high income landlords and low income tenants.

Both the Japanese example, and the differing degrees of leverage on corporate and non-corporate assets raise the possibility of changing the capital gains tax rules for some but not all assets. The original capital gains tax reform plan proposed by the Administration in 1989 would have reduced capital gains on corporate stocks but not on real estate investments. Similar plans have also been discussed in the Senate. Table 8 presents some information on the distributional consequences of reforms targeted at corporate stocks and at non-stock assets.

Two primary conclusions emerge. First, reductions in capital gains tax burdens on corporate stocks are more tilted toward those with high incomes than reductions in capital gains on non-stock assets. While nearly half of the benefits of a straight capital gains exclusion on non-stock assets would go to persons with incomes less than $100,000, only slightly more than one-fourth of the benefits of excluding capital gains on corporate stock would go to persons in the less-than-$100,000 income

TABLE 8
Cumulative Distributions of Capital Gains Relief: Stock and Non-Stock Assets

AGI breakpoints	Stock				Non Stock			
	Straight exclusion	Indexing	Sliding scale	Combination	Straight exclusion	Indexing	Sliding scale	Combination
0	2.44	1.74	2.38	2.17	3.21	2.15	2.78	2.62
2,500	2.55	2.04	2.48	2.33	3.38	2.47	2.93	2.86
6,000	3.47	3.22	3.16	3.07	4.71	4.46	4.05	4.53
12,000	4.82	6.00	4.40	5.09	7.86	9.68	7.32	8.89
20,000	6.45	9.8	5.35	7.22	13.5	17.6	11.7	14.8
25,000	8.08	14.6	6.84	9.87	16.8	22.6	15.1	19.1
30,000	9.03	16.5	7.86	11.2	20.6	28.5	18.5	24.1
40,000	13.5	21.4	11.4	15.1	30.6	38.7	29.9	34.7
50,000	15.9	25.4	13.7	17.8	39.3	52.11	39.4	45.9
75,000	27.7	42.1	25.2	30.1	50.4	65.6	50.4	58.0
100,000	34.1	49.8	30.5	35.7	61.1	74.2	60.9	67.7
200,000	52.7	71.4	50.7	56.2	76.8	86.7	76.5	81.3
500,000	74.1	88.6	71.0	75.4	88.8	95.6	88.4	91.5
1,000,000	84.2	94.0	81.6	84.6	93.6	97.8	93.1	95.2
1,000,000 +	100.0	100.0	100.0	100.0	100.0	100.0	100.0	100.0

Source: See Table 7.

class. Second, for both corporate stocks and other assets, it appears that indexing is relatively more favorable to lower income taxpayers. This suggests that the differing distributional consequences of indexation and exclusion do not arise from differences in the types of asset held by high and low income taxpayers but instead are the result of differences in the realization behavior of high and low income taxpayers.[3]

The results in this section suggest that a conflict between the goals of promoting economic efficiency and equity in the design of capital gains tax reform proposals. While measures targeted to corporate stocks are more defensible on efficiency grounds than measures targeted at non-stock assets, their benefits are less evenly distributed. While indexation is more progressive a reform than a capital gains exclusion, its benefits are tilted toward the types of assets that are most easily leveraged, so its efficiency consequences are far from clear. Of course, efficiency issues matter only insofar as capital gains reforms affect new investment as opposed to assets that are already in place. The next section takes up this issue.

III. CAPITAL GAINS TAX REFORM, NEW AND OLD INVESTMENT

An important objective of capital gains tax reform is stimulating investment by reducing the cost of capital. Only reforms which affect new investment can have this effect.[4] It is therefore interesting to gauge the share of the benefits of capital gains tax reductions that would apply to new as opposed to old capital. This depends on how long assets are held before being sold. If most realized capital gains occur on assets with long holding periods, then the share of the benefits of reform that go to new capital will be relatively low for the first few years after reform. The question of the length of the time that capital assets are held is also of interest because of concerns about the adverse consequences of "short-termism" in business planning.

Table 9 presents information on the share of capital gains on assets that have been held for varying lengths of time. Three conclusions emerge. First, most capital gains taxes are paid on assets that have been

[3] It is conceivable that differential returns on stock between high and low bracket taxpayers arise in part because low bracket taxpayers are more likely to hold high dividend stocks that pay relatively small capital gains.

[4] Fairness issues certainly arise when considering tax plans which favor new over old capital. They may be less serious in the current context than in other ones because of the substantial difference between the tax rates at which most assets held today were depreciated, and the tax rate levied at present.

TABLE 9
Cumulative Distributions of Benefits by Holding Period

Held less than	Straight exclusion	Indexing	Sliding scale	Combination
1 year	0.0	0.0	0.0	0.0
2	7.4	3.23	1.33	2.38
3	14.2	8.59	3.73	6.51
4	20.5	13.9	7.12	11.0
5	26.9	18.8	11.6	20.0
6	31.8	23.2	15.9	24.7
7	37.1	26.8	21.6	29.6
8	41.5	31.3	27.1	35.7
9	47.0	36.7	33.9	39.9
10	50.9	40.0	38.9	45.0
15	70.6	60.9	63.3	63.2
20	81.8	75.8	73.3	77.5
Beyond	100.0	100.0	100.0	100.0

Source: See Table 7.

held for a fairly long time. The figures in the table imply that more than half of all capital gains taxes are paid on assets that have been held for 10 years or more. Only a very small fraction (7.4 percent) of capital gains taxes are paid on assets that have been held for less than one year, and only one-fifth of capital gains taxes are paid on assets that have been held for less than four years. This implies that there is only very limited scope to discourage short term trading by raising the tax rate on short-term capital gains received by currently taxable investors. Indeed, the fact that reported short-term capital gains are typically negative suggests that such an approach might, by encouraging straddle-like strategies, actually increase the incidence of short term trading.

Second, a large fraction of the benefits of capital gains tax reductions would accrue to assets that were already in place at the time when a capital gains tax cut was enacted. For example, the table implies that even after five years, 75 percent of the benefits of an exclusion and 80 percent of the benefits of indexation would accrue to assets that were already in place when the reform was enacted. It is clear that virtually all of the benefits of a temporary capital gains tax cut would accrue to assets that had been purchased before the reform was enacted.

Third, there are modest differences between different reform plans in the extent to which long-term investments benefit. Because the sliding scale and the indexation options provide disproportionate relief to assets that have been held longer, their benefits are concentrated on holdings of long-term assets. Whereas half the benefits of a capital gains exclusion go to assets held more than 10 years, 60 percent of the benefits of indexing and 61 percent of the benefits of a sliding scale go to these assets. Perhaps the largest difference between the different plans is that the staggering and indexation options provide almost no relief to the small minority of assets that are sold in less than one year.

These estimates take no account of possible behavioral responses to a capital gains tax cut. To the extent that a capital gains tax cut stimulated realizations, they would be reinforced. The share of the benefit going to assets that had already been purchased increases if more of them were sold. Increasing the rate of realization necessarily implies reducing the horizon over which investors hold assets.

These estimates have a potentially important tax policy implication. They suggest that taxing only prospective capital gains would very significantly reduce the revenue cost of capital gains tax reform. In the short run, the revenue cost of indexing capital gains would be negligible as long as only prospective gains were to be indexed. Indeed, if taxpayers were required to realize gains on existing assets in order to qualify them for subsequent relief, prospective indexing might actually be a revenue raiser in the short run.

IV. CONCLUSIONS

The analysis in this paper has reached three main conclusions by looking at the distribution of the benefits associated with capital gains tax reductions. First, using plausible measures of economic status, capital gains receipts are highly concentrated among those with high incomes. The richest 2 percent of Americans receive more than 50 percent of all capital gains. Claims that capital gains recipients only appear to be rich because their capital gains income is transitory are not supported by longitudinal data. Likewise, claims that a large fraction of the benefits from capital gains tax reductions flow to middle income taxpayers result from failing to consider tax shelters. Capital gains on corporate stocks are considerably more concentrated among high income individuals than capital gains on other assets.

Second, there are important differences in the distributional consequences of different approaches to reducing capital gains taxes. Indexation yields greater benefits to lower income taxpayers than a general capital gains exclusion because they typically hold assets longer before selling them, and because they typically enjoy smaller gains than higher income taxpayers. Indexation also favors real estate over corporate stocks to a much greater extent than does a general exclusion. A sliding scale capital gains tax cut, based on the amount of time an asset is held has distributional consequences very similar to a general exclusion.

Third, most capital gains are realized on assets that were held for 10 or more years. Reductions in capital gains taxes would, for many years, benefit primarily assets that are already in place. This is especially true of indexing and sliding scale plans. Confining capital gains tax relief to future gains would substantially reduce the revenue cost of capital gains reform.

The statistical work in the paper all assumes that there are no behavioral responses to changes in tax rates, an assumption which is surely unwarranted. However, it is unlikely that taking account of behavioral responses would alter the conclusions. Unless reductions in capital gains taxes would have a larger effect on realizations for lower than higher income taxpayers, taking account of behavioral effects would operate to strengthen the conclusion that capital gains tax reduction would primarily benefit high income taxpayers. Since they always have the option of not changing their realization strategy, any induced realizations following a tax cut are an indication that taxpayers are better off even if they do pay more in taxes. Conclusions about which assets would benefit most from capital gains tax reductions are probably not very sensitive to changes in behavior. And the conclusion that most of the benefits of capital gains cuts would go to assets that are already in place would be reinforced if behavioral effects were considered.

A broader argument challenging the results in this paper might assert that our assessment of the effects of capital gains cuts neglects the consequences of increased investment. Increased investment, it is argued would raise the productivity of labor and so raise wages, and by spurring capital accumulation would reduce pre-tax returns to capital. There is no question that such a general equilibrium effect of capital gains tax reductions would operate to make them more progressive. However, we are skeptical that this qualification is very important for our conclusions. First, as we have noted, most of the benefits of capital gains tax reductions go to old capital and so do not have incentive effects. Any favorable incentive effects on new capital are mitigated by the taxpayers' realization that the tax could be reformed yet again. Second, available estimates such as those of the Treasury's 1985 study suggest that reducing capital gains taxes would have only a negligible impact on long-term capital accumulation. To the extent that tax cuts would encourage real estate investments, it is questionable how much they would raise workers' productivity or wages. Third, capital gains tax reductions probably operate to increase the demand for capital but to reduce its supply. This is because they encourage individuals to sell capital assets, which may encourage them to spend the proceeds. To this extent, the impact of capital gains tax reductions on capital accumulation is ambiguous.

The analysis here highlights the conflicts inherent in designing a capital gains tax reform principle. The simplest reform, bringing back a partial capital gains exclusion benefits corporate stocks but is the most regressive of the reforms considered. Indexing on the other hand is progressive in its incidence but primarily benefits real estate and so may not increase the neutrality of the tax system. Indexing also favors old over new capital. The resolution of these conflicts as well as broader conflicts over the desirability of any type of capital gains tax reform will depend on the values policy makers attach to differing objectives as well as how they resolve judgments about the likely behavioral effect of tax changes.

APPENDIX

Three separate micro data files were used in the preparation of this study. All are public use samples of actual tax return data, as filed with the Internal Revenue Service.

The Individual Income Tax Model is a stratified random sample of individual income tax returns. High income returns are greatly over-sampled (with sampling rates as high as one in three) and this enhances the usefulness of the file for a study of capital gains realizations. Weights are provided to reproduce the universe of taxpayers. The information included covers almost the complete Form 1040, but only a few items from each supporting schedule and only two—long and short net gains—from the Schedule D. No demographic data (such as age, race, or sex) are available, and even the age exemption is suppressed on returns with over $100,000. It has 75,400 records.

The panel file used in Section I is a non-stratified random sample of individual income tax returns for the years 1979 through 1984. This is a longitudinal sample in which individual taxpayers appear repeatedly. Because high income returns are not oversampled, and the sample size is smaller, this file is not ideal for capital gains studies. Returns are included in the panel according to the last four digits of the primary taxpayer's social security number. In 1979–1981 five specific four-digit endings qualified a return for selection, yielding about 46,000 returns per year. In 1982 and 1984 budget stringency reduced the sample to a single four-digit ending and in 1983 to two such endings. Only one return per year was sampled, so a taxpayer filing late one year would not be included unless he or she continued to file late in subsequent years.

This unusual sampling scheme has a number of consequences. First, new taxpayers may enter the sample in any year. Second, taxpayers may enter and leave the sample at random according to the sampling rate each year or systematically according to their filing status. Third, women (who are rarely primary taxpayers on joint returns) leave the sample on marriage and reenter on divorce or widowhood.

For Table 2, six years of data are pooled. Out of 177,177 total returns, 92,146 belong to 15,384 taxpayers with four or more years of data available. Only these taxpayers are used. Because this selection process is non-random, the resulting tables are not directly comparable to the tax model files discussed above.

The 1973 Sales of Capital Assets file is the only file of individual transactions available for public use. It forms the basis for all our analysis of capital gains on different types of capital assets. The file contains about 415,000 (only 151,818 are usable) records of individual sales transactions as reported on Form 1040 Schedule D, Form 4797 and Form 2119 by 54,658 taxpayers with capital asset sales reported on calendar year 1973. For each transaction, the kind of property, purchase and sale dates, basis, selling price, and adjustments are given. In contrast to the other files used here, data are missing for a significant number of transactions. About 5 percent of transactions records lack purchase or sale price, and about 25 percent lack the purchase date. Suspiciously, the purchase date and month is always present if the purchase year is present. For transactions characterized as short-term gains by the taxpayer, we have assumed a six-month holding period if no purchase date was provided. 151,818 Schedule D transactions for taxpayers with net gains are retained.

A separate file gives taxpayer information from the 1973 Individual Income Tax Model, and this can be linked to the transaction data. This provides essentially the same information available in the Individual Tax Model Files for later years, but only covers taxpayers with capital asset transactions. The 1986 Tax Model File (aged to 1989 levels) was used to generate average tax rates by AGI class for capital gains recipients.

In all cases, dollar values are expressed in 1989 dollars. Aging of income flows to 1989 dollars was done using as a deflator, the change in per (adult) capita disposable income less transfers. In applying Fisher's law to the 1973 data to simulate recent inflation experience, we used the personal consumption deflator as a measure of inflation.

REFERENCES

Avery, Robert B. and Gregory E. Elliehausen. 1986. Financial Characteristics of High-Income Families. *Federal Reserve Bulletin* 72: 163–75.

Congressional Budget Office. 1989. The Distribution of Benefits From a Reduction in the Tax Rate on Capital Gains. Staff Memorandum, October.

Gordon, Roger H., James R. Hines, Jr., and Lawrence H. Summers. 1987. Notes on the Tax Treatment of Structures. In *The Effects of Taxation on Capital Accumulation*, M. Feldstein, ed. Chicago: University of Chicago Press.

Internal Revenue Service. Undated. General Description Booklet for the 1986 Individual Public Use Tax File. Washington, D.C.

Poterba, James M. 1989. Venture Capital and Capital Gains Taxation. In *Tax Policy and the Economy* 3, L. Summers, ed. Cambridge: NBER and MIT Press.

Shoven, John B. 1989. The Japanese Tax Reform and the Effective Rate of Tax on Japanese Corporate Investments. In *Tax Policy and the Economy 3*, L. Summers, ed. Cambridge: NBER and MIT Press.

Slemrod, Joel, Laura Kalambokidis, and William Shobe. 1989. Who Realizes Capital Gains? *Tax Notes*, October 23.

Slemrod, Joel, 1988. The 1979–84 Linked Panel of Tax Return Data: Sampling and Linking Methodology. (unpublished memorandum, University of Michigan Business School).

Summers, Lawrence H. 1981. Inflation, the Stock Market, and Owner-Occupied Housing. *American Economic Review* 71: 429–34.

———. 1987. Should Tax Reform Level the Playing Field? *NTA-TIA Proceedings of the 79th Annual Conference*, 119–24. Columbus, Ohio: NTA-TIA.

Yitzhaki, Shlomo. 1987. The Relation Between Return and Income. *Quarterly Journal of Economics* 102: 77–95.

TREATMENT OF CAPITAL INCOME IN RECENT TAX REFORMS AND THE COST OF CAPITAL IN INDUSTRIALIZED COUNTRIES

Eytan Sheshinski
Hebrew University and Columbia University

I. INTRODUCTION

Following the 1986 Tax Reform Act in the United States, the tax systems of most industrial countries are undergoing, or have already carried out, significant changes. The countries where major reforms are being or have been enacted are Australia, Japan, Denmark, and New Zealand. Less drastic reforms are being or have been enacted in France, Germany, Italy, Belgium, Sweden, Norway, the Netherlands, and a few others. On the basis of a worldwide study, Pechman (1987) concludes that these countries have been "impressed by the success of tax reform in the United States, particularly the reduction in the top income tax rate" (p. 1). More important, perhaps, is the widespread discontent with existing tax systems, which are seen to cause serious inequities and misallocations.

In both the individual and the corporate income tax, the predominant principles in these tax reforms were a reduction of the statutory rates and a broadening of the taxable base. In terms of the overall tax burden, these principles work in opposite directions. Although all these reforms were supposed to be "revenue neutral," i.e., to make tax revenues no greater or lower, they clearly have equity and efficiency effects which should be examined. While the schedular changes and base broadening with regard to labor earnings have been fairly widely documented (see, for example, Pechman, 1987, and Tanzi, 1987) the changes with regard to the taxation of capital income—interest, dividends and capital gains—have been less clear. One reason is the complexity of the laws, even after tax reform, pertaining to corporate income, withholding at source, and short- and long-term capital gains. Another reason is the need to distinguish between nominal and real tax rates. Tax systems which include nominal interest income and allow deductions of nominal interest expenses in the taxable base are not neutral with respect to price changes. That is, effective real tax rates vary with the rate of inflation. In the absence of indexation, the same applies to capital gains. All industrial countries have experienced in recent years a decline in the rate of inflation. A major objective of this paper is to evaluate the impact of these combined changes—reduction in tax rates coupled with elimination of many tax expenditures and a decline in the rate of inflation—on the cost of capital.

II. THE U.S. TAX REFORM

It would not be possible in this paper to give details of the 1986 Tax Reform Act, but the essential elements can be listed:

1. Personal exemptions and standard deductions have been doubled, thereby removing five million people, officially defined as "poor," from the tax rolls. The principle that the poor should not be taxed, as well as the distribution of the tax burden, will be maintained by the automatic adjustment of brackets and personal exemptions to inflation;
2. Increases in the earned income credit for wage earners with families eliminated almost the entire social security tax for those eligible for full credit and decreased the tax burden for low income earners.
3. The new rate structure has four brackets, with rates of 15, 28, 33 and 28 percent, replacing the earlier 14 rates which rose to a maximum of 50 percent. The 33 percent bracket reflects the phasing out, at a 5 percent rate, of the benefits of the lowest tax rate and the personal exemptions.
4. Capital gains are taxed as ordinary income, reflecting the adoption of

the "comprehensive income" concept for tax purposes. The absence of indexation of nominal capital gains on the one hand, and the continued exemption of accrued capital gains on assets transferred by gift or at death on the other, affect the real burden and the economic impact of the tax in opposite directions.

5. Broad elimination of major loopholes, tax shelters, and special benefits. For example, unemployment benefits which were previously taxable only if a married taxpayer's annual income exceeded $18,000 ($12,000 for singles) were made taxable regardless of size. Deductions for state and local sales taxes and consumer interest were eliminated. Deductions for unreimbursed business expenses and other miscellaneous expenses were allowed only to the extent that they exceed two percent of income.

6. A limitation was imposed on the deductibility of losses from passive investments, thereby eliminating many tax shelters. The deduction of interest expenses for investment was limited to the amount of investment income. Minimum tax floors for individuals and businesses were strengthened.

7. The corporate income tax rate was reduced from 46 to 34 percent. The tax on dividends was thereby cut from a maximum of 73 to 52.5 percent. On the other hand, elimination of the investment tax credit and the reduction in depreciation allowances (for structures) has broadened the corporate taxable base. The overall outcome is an increase of 20 percent in corporate tax liabilities.

The distributional impact of all these changes has been estimated by Pechman (1989) to be highly progressive.

III. TAX REFORMS IN OTHER COUNTRIES

A large number of industrial countries have followed the United States and have enacted, or are in the process of adopting, major tax reforms. Although the extent and details vary across countries, some common trends can be observed.

1. Reduction in individual tax rates, particularly in the top brackets, and a compression in the number of brackets. Table 1 shows that between 1985 and 1987 the top marginal tax rate was reduced on average from 66 to 56 percent, i.e., a reduction of 16 percent. Leading the list is New Zealand (26 points and scheduled to decline 8 additional points by 1993!), Japan (23 points), as compared with a 22 point reduction in the United States, 10 points in the United Kingdom and 11 points in Au-

TABLE 1
Marginal Tax Rates and Number of Brackets

| | Marginal tax rates[a] | | | | | | Number of brackets | |
| | 1985 | | 1987 | | 1989 | | | |
Countries	lowest	highest	lowest	highest	lowest	highest	1985	1989
United States	11	55[b]	15	43	15	33	15	2–3
Canada	—	52[c]	—	53	—	48	—	—
Australia	30	60	24	49	24	49	5	4
Japan	10	88	10	76	10	65	15	6
New Zealand	20	66	15	48	15	40	5	3
Denmark	50	73	50	68	50	68	—	—
France	5	65	5	57	5	57	—	—
Germany	22	56	19	56	19	56	—	—
Italy	18	62	11	62	11	62	9	8
The Netherlands	—	72	—	72	—	72	9	3–4
Sweden	—	80[d]	—	77	—	72	16	3
United Kingdom	30	60	27	60	27	50	—	—
Average	22	66	20	60	20	56	11	4

Source: Pechman (1987, p. 4), supplemented by Pechman (1989) and Vito Tanzi (1987).

[a] Combined national and local tax rates.

[b] Takes into account the deductibility of local tax when calculating national tax.

[c] Includes federal and provincial surtaxes (and the Ontario provincial tax rate).

[d] Assumes local tax rate of 30 percent.

stralia. However, no country has gone as far as the United States in terms of the level of the top marginal tax rate. Futhermore, the relative spread between the top marginal rates across countries has somewhat increased (the coefficient of variation is 0.16 in 1985 and 0.21 in 1989). Further attempts toward rate uniformity are expected to take place in the Common Market and elsewhere after 1992. The persistence of these tax differentials may provide an inducement for highly skilled labor migration from high to low tax countries. Although the percentage of individuals at the highest rate may be small,[1] such a "brain drain" may have a significant impact.

2. Tax treatment of income from capital varies significantly across countries. As seen in Table 2, only Germany and the Netherlands tax interest income at the same rate as earnings. In the United Kingdom and

[1] Tanzi (1987) provides OECD data pertaining to 1981, showing that the top tax rate applies to less than 1 percent of taxpayers, but the percentage of tax yields from these taxpayers was between 4–8 percent of total tax revenues. The widening of the brackets after tax reforms has undoubtedly increased the numbers of the taxpayers at the top rate.

TABLE 2

Tax Rates on Capital Income in Selected Countries, 1989

Countries	Interest		Dividends			Top marginal rate on long term capital gains
	Rate of withholding on bonds	Top marginal tax rate or–if withholding is final	Rate of withholding	Top marginal rate or–if withholding is final		
Denmark	0	40	30	40		0[d]
France	26[a]	—	0	57		16[e]
Germany	0	56/53[c]	25	56/53[c]		0[f]
Italy	12.5	—	10	56/53[c]		0
The Netherlands	0	72/60[c]	25	72/60[c]		0
United Kingdom	0–25[b]	40	0	40		30[g]

Source: Conceil National du Credit: Lebeque Report, IMF, OECD.

[a] Including 1 percent social security contribution.

[b] Zero rate for certain public loans.

[c] Current rate and proposed rate for 1990, respectively.

[d] Stocks held over three years and bonds.

[e] If transactions do not exceed F 288,400, capital gains are exempt.

[f] Assets held over six months.

[g] A £4,000 exemption applies.

in Denmark the top marginal tax rate on interest is 40 percent, while on wage earnings it is 50 percent. In France and in Italy interest income is taxed at its source, at flat rates of 26 percent and 12.5 percent, respectively. The proposed tax reform in Japan also taxes interest income at a uniform 20 percent rate. This tendency to tax financial income at lower, and sometimes uniform, rates is less pronounced when it comes to dividends. As a rule, long-term capital gains are not taxed, or taxed at a significantly lower marginal tax rate (France and the United Kingdom).

There is a striking difference between these countries and the United States. While the 1986 Tax Reform Act in the United States has moved towards a comprehensive income concept in taxing equally all sources of income, there is no discernible trend in this direction among the European countries.

Tanzi (1987) notes that "while there is a lot of similarity in the way countries tax interest incomes, there are wide differences in the way they have been treating interest expenses." His data indicate that Denmark, Finland, Luxembourg, the Netherlands, Norway, Sweden, and the United States were by far the most generous in allowing wide deductibility for interest expenses. On the other hand, Canada, France, Germany, Italy, Japan, the United Kingdom and some other countries were far less generous.

The recent tax reforms have, however, reduced the differences among these countries. For example, before 1986, the United States fully taxed nominal interest incomes of individuals and allowed unlimited deductibility for all interest payments. Japan, on the other hand, exempted interest income and limited interest deductions (for example, for a second residence and on consumer loans. Even the deduction for principal residence mortgage had a low ceiling.) As already noted, the 1986 Tax Reform Act in the United States is phasing out the deductibility of interest expenses, while in Japan a 1987 law extended mortgage deductions in the middle income range; their tax reform in 1988 includes a 20 percent tax on interest income.

3. Corporate tax rates in other countries are also declining, but less drastically than the tax rates on individuals. The average corporate tax rate has declined from 49 percent in 1985 to 43 percent in 1989. New Zealand has the lowest rate (28 percent), the United Kingdom and the Netherlands second (35 percent) and the United States, Australia, and France are third (39 percent). Japan plans a further reduction (to 40 percent) in 1990, and Sweden (to 40 percent) in 1991.

There also seems to be a great deal of uniformity in the European corporate tax systems regarding allowance for depreciation and loss carryover regulations (Table 3). The United States is significantly more

TABLE 3
Depreciation and Loss Carryover in Corporate Tax Systems

Countries	Lifetime for tax purposes		Loss carryover	
	Machinery	Buildings	Carry forward	Carry backward
United States	3–10	15–20	15	3
Denmark	10	30	5	0
France	10	20	5	0
Germany	10	25	5	2
Italy	8.5	21.3	5	0
The Netherlands	10	33	8	3
United Kingdom	–a	25	No limit	1

Source: International Bureau of Fiscal Documentation, OECD, Paris, Price Waterhouse.

a Declining balance method with a 25 percent rate.

generous in allowing faster depreciation rates and carryover losses both backward and forward.[2]

In reducing investment tax incentives, the United Kingdom led the way in 1984 by eliminating expensing for plant and equipment, using the tax revenues to reduce the corporate rate from 50 to 40 and then 35 percent. The United States and Canada have also eliminated the investment tax credit and reduced the corporate tax rate. Australia has temporarily increased its corporate tax rate but this should be partially offset by relief for dividends received by stockholders. The countries with high corporate tax rates—Germany, Japan, Sweden, and Denmark—may have to reduce their rates to be competitive in international markets.

The combined effect of base-broadening and rate reduction has been on average to keep corporate tax revenues intact, i.e., revenue neutral (Table 4).

4. There are major differences between countries with respect to capital gains taxation of traded stocks. Only the United States and Australia regard capital gains as ordinary income, i.e., tax these gains at the same rate as earnings. All other countries either fully exempt or tax at extremely favorable rates long-term gains (i.e., gains on stocks held longer than a year, or, in Sweden, longer than two years) (Table 5). Pechman (1989) thinks that "this attitude reflects the long standing European view that capital gains are not income." These countries also doubt the possi-

---

[2] After 1986, the depreciation method for equipment is the declining balance (at 200 percent) or straight line, whichever provides the maximum deduction, and declining balance (at 150 percent) on structures.

TABLE 4
Corporate Income Tax Rates and Tax Revenues As Percent
of Total Tax Receipts

Countries	Corporate income tax rates[a]			Corporate income tax revenues as percent of total tax receipts	
	1985	1987	1989	1980	1987
United States	51	45	39	10	8
Canada[b]	52	52	44	12	8
Australia	46	49	39	12	10
Japan[c,d]	55	55	53	22	21
New Zealand	45	48	28	8	9
Denmark	50	50	50	3	4
France[c]	50	45	39	5	5
Germany	56	56	56	5	5
Italy	46	46	46	8	4
The Netherlands	43	42	35	7	8
Sweden	52	52	52	2	4
United Kingdom	40	35	35	8	11
Average	49	44	43	8	8

Source: Corporate Tax Rates: Pechman (1987, p. 5), supplemented in Pechman (1989); Corporate Tax Revenues: OECD, Committee on Fiscal Affairs, DAFFFE/CFA/89.14.

[a] Combined national and local tax rates.

[b] Tax rate for non-manufacturing corporation. Tax for a manufacturing corporation is lower.

[c] Tax on undistributed profits only. Tax on distributed profits taxed at lower rate in Germany and Japan and at a higher rate in France (beginning in 1989).

[d] Takes into account the deductibility of local tax from national tax.

bility of restricting the deduction for net capital losses, as imposed by the United States ($3,000 annually).

Except Australia, no country that taxes capital gains has adopted indexation of the buying value.

IV. INTEREST INCOME TAXATION, INFLATION, AND THE REAL COST OF CAPITAL

The major factors in the tax system that distort the lending-borrowing decisions are its treatment of interest income and the deductibility of interest expenses. In the presence of inflation, it is particularly important whether the tax system distinguishes between *nominal* and *real* in-

TABLE 5
Individual Taxation of Capital Gains on Portfolio Stock Investments, 1989

Country	Maximum short-term capital gain tax rate (percent)[a]	Maximum long-term capital gain tax rate (percent)[a]	Period to qualify for long-term gain treatment	Maximum annual net worth tax rate (percent)
United States[b]	33.0	33.0	One year	None
Australia[c]	50.3	50.3	One year	None
Belgium	Exempt	Exempt	None	None
Canada[d]	17.5	17.5	None	None
France[e]	16.0	16.0	None	None
Germany[f]	56.0	Exempt	Six months	0.5
Italy	Exempt	Exempt	None	None
Japan[g]	5.0	5.0	None	None
The Netherlands	Exempt	Exempt	None	0.8
Sweden	45.0	18.0	Two years	3.0
United Kingdom[h]	40.0	40.0	None	None

Source: C. Walker and M. Bloomfield, "The Case for the Restoration of a Capital Gains Tax Differential," *Tax Notes*, May 22, 1989, p. 1021.

[a] State, provincial, and local taxes are not included. They can in some cases be substantial. Furthermore, in some countries exclusion rules might apply.

[b] The nominal tax rate for long- and short-term capital gains is 28 percent. The marginal rate, however, rises to 33 percent for joint returns between $74,850 and $155,370 and for single returns between $44,900 and $93,130 for calendar year 1989.

[c] Indexing is allowed on long-term capital gains.

[d] Canadian residents are allowed an annual capital gains exemption of Can $30,000 subject to a cumulative exemption of up to Can$500,000. In 1990, the lifetime capital gains exemption is reduced to $100,000, except for owner/operators of farms and small business corporations who may continue to apply the $500,000 limit.

[e] Gains from proceeds of up to F 272,000 are exempt from taxation in a given taxable year.

[f] The first DM 1,000 of short-term capital gains is exempt from tax.

[g] Japan's tax reform plan, which took effect in 1989, imposes a maximum tax of approximately 5 percent on the sale of securities.

[h] Only gains and losses accrued since 1982 may still be taxed; gains since 1982 are indexed.

terest. In the absence of taxes on interest, the nominal rate of interest has to increase by the rate of inflation in order to keep the real rate of interest unchanged. When nominal interest incomes are taxed and nominal interest payments are deductible expenses, the increase in the nominal rate of interest, r, is related to the real rate of interest, r^*, to the rate of inflation, Π, and to the rate of interest taxation, t, by the well-known formula:

$$r = r^* + \frac{\Pi}{1 - t} \tag{1}$$

The rate r is sometimes called the *"required"* rate of interest (Tanzi, 1987).

As seen in Table 6, the rate of inflation in the 1980s has decreased in all industrial countries. While the average rate of inflation has been 12.5 percent in 1980, it came down to 3.5 percent in 1987. As we have seen, tax rates also decreased during the same period. Both of these factors worked to reduce the required rates of interest. It is interesting to inquire whether these rates have conformed with formula (1), keeping the real rates of interest invariant.

In Table 7 we have calculated the "required" interest rates in different countries during 1980–1989, using the data on rates of inflation (Table 6) and on tax rates (Table 1); under the assumption that the real rate of interest is 4 percent. As expected, the average of the "required" rates declined significantly during this period, from 22.2 percent in 1985 to 12.8 percent in 1989, i.e., a decline of 9 percent. The bulk of this decline (about 70 percent) is due to the decrease in inflation rates, the rest is due to the reduction in tax rates.

Did the actual interest rates change to the same extent as the "required" rates? If changes in the actual rates of interest were less or more accentuated than those in the required rates, this implies that the real rates facing lenders and borrowers were not invariant.

TABLE 6
Inflation Rates in Industrial Countries Undergoing Tax Reform

Countries	Inflation rates (consumer prices)			
	1980	1983	1985	1987
United States	13.5	3.2	3.6	3.7
Canada	10.2	5.8	4.0	4.4
Australia	10.1	10.1	6.7	8.5
Japan	8.0	1.9	2.0	—
New Zealand	17.2	7.4	15.4	12.3
Denmark	12.3	6.9	4.7	4.0
France	13.3	9.6	5.8	3.3
Germany	5.4	3.3	2.2	0.3
Italy	21.2	14.6	9.2	4.7
The Netherlands	6.5	7.8	2.2	−0.5
Sweden	13.7	8.9	9.4	4.2
United Kingdom	18.0	4.6	6.1	4.2
Average	12.5	7.0	5.9	3.5

Source: Inflation Rates—IMF, *International Financial Statistics, 1988.*

TABLE 7

"Required" and Actual Interest Rates in Industrial Countries Undergoing Tax Reforms

	"Required" interest rates[a]					Deposit rates			Lending rates		
	1980[b]	1983[b]	1985	1987	1989[c]	1985	1987	1989	1985	1987	1989
United States	34.0	11.1	12.0	10.5	9.5	8.05	6.86	6.72	9.93	8.21	8.59
Canada	25.3	16.1	12.3	13.4	12.5	8.46	7.66	8.44[d]	10.58	9.52	9.75
Australia	29.3	29.3	20.8	20.7	20.7	10.46	13.77	11.50	15.96	19.83	18.08
Japan	70.7	19.8	20.7	4.0	4.0	3.50	1.76	1.76	6.52	5.09	4.92
New Zealand	54.6	25.8	49.3	27.7	24.5	14.71	18.42	—	—	—	—
Denmark	49.6	29.6	21.4	16.5	16.5	8.21	7.03	—	14.65	14.17	—
France	42.0	31.4	20.6	11.7	11.7	6.80	5.31	4.90	17.77	15.82	15.80
Germany	16.3	11.5	9.0	4.7	4.7	4.44	3.20	2.78	9.53	8.36	8.07
Italy	59.8	42.4	28.2	16.4	16.4	10.90	7.02	6.60	18.15	13.57	13.50
The Netherlands	27.2	14.0	11.9	2.2	2.2	4.10	3.55	3.45	9.25	8.15	7.00
Sweden	72.5	48.5	41.0	22.3	19.0	11.83	8.94	8.75	16.72	12.99	13.14
United Kingdom	49.0	15.5	19.3	14.5	12.4	8.87	5.35	3.72	12.29	9.63	8.67

Source: Deposit and Lending Rates, IMF, *International Financial Statistics*, 1988, p. 68.

[a] Required interest rate $= 4 + \dfrac{\text{Inflation rate}}{1 - \text{top marginal tax rate}}$.

Data from Tables 1 and 6.

[b] Assuming tax rates as in 1985.

[c] Assuming inflation rate as in 1987.

[d] 1987, IV.

Table 7 also provides data on deposit and lending interest rates during 1985–1988. As expected, these rates declined significantly (average lending rates, for example, went down from 12.9 percent in 1985 to 10.7 percent in 1988), but not to the same extent as the required rates. In fact, a linear regression of the required rates, r, on lending rates, r_1, yields

$$r = -2.17 + 1.43 \, r_1 \quad (R^2 = 0.52) \quad (2)$$
$$(1.85) \quad (0.25)$$

A coefficient of 1.43 (highly significant with 32 observations) and insignificant intercepts imply that actual interest rates adjust *only partially* (about 0.7 of a percentage point for each 1 percentage point) to changes in the required rates. This means that the decline in the tax rates and in the rate of inflation had a *real* effect toward reducing real interest rates.

A direct way to measure the effect of the tax on interest income is to calculate the effective real marginal tax rate for recipients of interest income:

$$\text{effective real marginal tax rate} = \frac{r_1 t}{r_1 - \Pi} \quad (3)$$

where t was taken as the top individual marginal tax rate. These calculations are presented in Table 8. In 1989, the United States had the lowest real tax rate, while in 1985, Germany had the lowest rate. It should be emphasized that these are the tax rates that would apply if interest income was taxed as ordinary income, as is the case in the United States. Japan, for example, did not tax interest income until 1989 and will now tax it at a flat 20 percent rate.

More significant, presumably, is a comparison of the real rates faced by borrowers who can deduct nominal interest expenses. A major reason for the attention in recent years to the tax treatment of interest expenses has been the combination of high inflation rates and the unlimited deductibility of nominal interest expenses. As Tanzi (1987) notes, after-tax interest rates were negative for many taxpayers, creating an inducement for consumption and low savings. He notes that in Denmark, for instance, in 1985 interest deductions by individuals were 16 percent of personal income. For many individuals these deductions could be taken against marginal tax rates of 73 percent.

As a result, Denmark now limits the tax rate against which interest deductions are allowed to 50 percent. Similar negative effects of interest deductions were felt in the other Scandinavian countries and reforms were undertaken reducing the advantages of borrowing. Dividing coun-

TABLE 8

Real Interest Rates, Effective Real Marginal Tax Rates on Interest Income, and Real Borrowing Rates

Countries	Real interest rates[a]		Effective real marginal tax rates[b]		Real borrowing rates[c]	
	1985	1989	1985	1989	1985	1987
United States	6.3	4.9	86.3	58.0	0.9	2.1
Canada	6.6	5.4	83.6	87.5	1.1	0.7
Australia	9.3	9.6	103.4	92.5	−0.3	0.7
Japan	4.5	4.9	127.0	65.0	−1.2	1.7
New Zealand	—	—	—	—	—	—
Denmark	10.0	—	107.5	—	−0.7	—
France	12.0	12.5	96.5	72.0	0.4	3.5
Germany	7.3	7.8	72.8	58.2	2.0	3.3
Italy	9.0	8.8	125.7	95.1	−2.3	0.4
The Netherlands	7.1	7.5	94.5	67.2	0.4	2.5
Sweden	9.3	8.9	143.5	105.8	−4.1	−0.5
United Kingdom	6.2	4.5	119.1	97.0	−1.2	0.1

[a] Lending Rate − Inflation rate

[b] $\dfrac{\text{Lending Rate}}{\text{Real Interest Rate}} \times \text{Marginal Tax Rate}$

[c] Lending Rate (1 − Marginal Tax Rate) − Inflation Rate

tries into those with the most generous treatment and those with the least generous treatment of interest deductions, Tanzi (1987) finds that household savings out of disposable income has been significantly lower in the former group (an average of 4 percent vs. 9 percent in 1985).

Table 8 indicates that the decrease in the rates of inflation and the reduction in marginal tax rates has increased the average real borrowing rate of interest from −0.5 percent in 1985 to 1.5 percent in 1987. The United States rate in 1987 was higher than in Japan (1.7) and the United Kingdom (0.1) but lower than in France (3.5) and Germany (3.3).

V. EVALUATING THE EFFICIENCY GAINS FROM LOWER TAXES ON CAPITAL INCOME

The previous discussion has demonstrated that in most countries, capital income is taxed at preferentially low rates. While in the United States the equalization of tax rates on ordinary income and capital gains has been a keystone of the tax reform, no such tendency is evident in other countries. This, and the recent debate in the United States on rolling back capital gains taxation to a maximum of 15 percent, raised the natural question of whether such differential tax rates are efficient.

Economists have long been aware that, from an efficiency point of view, comprehensive income taxation will be the exception rather than the rule. Models that attempt to determine the optimal structure of income tax rates on earnings and on income from capital, depending on labor supply and on savings elasticities, rarely give rise to equal tax rates. Actually, some of the most commonly used models justify *no* taxation of capital income, i.e., taxation of earnings and an exemption for capital income (see, for example, Sheshinksi, 1989, and the references therein). Even in these circumstances, however, equity considerations may induce some taxation of capital. While a detailed analysis of this issue is clearly beyond the objectives of this paper, it seems worthwhile to provide some evaluation of the welfare gains obtained in moving to lower tax rates on capital income.

Feldstein (1978) has shown that the gains of a shift from equal tax rates on capital and labor to an income tax imposed only on labor earnings (keeping tax revenues intact) are equal between 2 and 2.5 percent of total labor income in the United States. This is a major efficiency gain.

We have adopted the elasticities assumed by Feldstein: labor supply wage elasticity of .3 and a savings elasticity with respect to the interest rate of .07, and have shown (Appendix) that the efficiency gains are somewhat about 1.2 percent of total labor income—and, more important, that 80 percent of this welfare gain is obtained by reducing the capital income tax to *half* the rate of the tax on earnings. Thus, while a departure from comprehensive income taxation toward lower taxation of capital income may lead to substantial welfare gains, most of these gains are obtained before a 2:1 ratio of labor to capital income rates are attained, and welfare is quite insensitive to further reductions in capital taxation (accompanied by an increase in labor taxation).

VI. CONCLUDING REMARKS

This paper has surveyed the major trends in tax reforms in industrial countries, particularly in relation to the taxation of income from capital—interest, dividends, and capital gains. It has been demonstrated that, while reforms concerning the tax treatment of earnings have a common tendency to reduce marginal rates, particularly the top rates, coupled with a broadening of the tax base ("leveling the playing field"), no such tendency is observed with regard to the taxation of income from capital. No other country has adopted the comprehensive income concept, which underlies the United States' 1986 Tax Reform Act. Without exception, interest income and, to a lesser extent, dividends are taxed at favorably low rates (including zero) and long-term capital gains are, as a rule, exempt.

All tax systems have avoided indexing capital income to changes in the price level. As a consequence, the presence of high and variable inflation rates has been a major source of distortion in the capital markets. In spite of reductions in marginal tax rates, net rates of return to lenders have been negatively affected by inflation, i.e., actual nominal rates have not fully compensated for inflation and lagged behind the rates "required" to preserve the real rates. The nominal basis has also been the major factor that prevented a convergence of effective real tax rates across countries.

Faced with negative or very low real interest rates for borrowers, many countries attempt to curb the negative effect on household savings by imposing limits on interest deductibility.

The Scandinavian practice of taxing *net* capital income at the lowest marginal rates in the individual income tax schedule is similar in spirit to the proposed flat tax rate (20 percent) on interest income proposed in Japan and Israel.

Adjustments of interest and capital gains for inflation and the use of real economic depreciation seem to be the best method to eliminate most of the tax benefits of tax shelters. Furthermore, indexation is a necessary condition for further harmonization of tax rates in different countries.

APPENDIX

We wish to analyze the welfare cost of capital income taxation relative to labor income. Following Feldstein (1978) and Green and Sheshinsky (1979), consider a two-period model, in which labor supply in the first period is variable and the individual's second-period consumption is the after-tax value of his savings. Two tax rates are to be selected: a tax on labor earnings and a tax on interest income. Individuals are assumed to maximize

$$U(c_1, c_2, 1 - L) = \alpha \log c_1 + \beta \log c_2 + \gamma \log (1 - L) \qquad \text{(A.1)}$$

subject to

$$c_1 + \frac{c_2}{1 + r} - wL = 0 \qquad \text{(A.2)}$$

where c_1 = first-period consumption; c_2 = second-period (retirement) consumption; $1 - L$ = leisure in the first period; r = net (after-tax) interest rate; w = net (after-tax) wage rate, in units of c_1. The non-negative constants α, β and γ can be chosen, without loss of generality, to satisfy $\alpha + \beta + \gamma = 1$. The expenditure function, E, associated with (A.1) is

$$E(w,r,u) = A(1 + r)^{-\beta}w^{\gamma}e^{u} - w \qquad \text{(A.3)}$$

where $A = \alpha^{-\alpha}\beta^{-\beta}\gamma^{-\gamma}$. Compensated demands are given by the partial derivatives of E w.r.t. prices. The price of second-period consumption is $1/(1 + r)$ and the price of leisure is w. Thus,

$$c_1 = \alpha A(1 + r)^{-\beta}w^{\gamma}e^{u}$$

$$c_2 = \beta A(1 + r)^{-\beta}w^{\gamma}e^{u}$$

$$1 - L = \gamma A(1 + r)^{-\beta}w^{\gamma-1}e^{u} \qquad \text{(A.4)}$$

where c_1 is obtained from the identity $E = c_1 + \dfrac{c_2}{1 + r} - wL$.

There are two (ad valorem) taxes: an earnings tax at the rate τ, and a capital income tax at a rate t. Thus, net returns are related to gross returns $\bar{r}$ and $\bar{w}$ by

$$r = \bar{r}(1 - t)$$
$$w = \bar{w}(1 - \tau). \qquad \text{(A.5)}$$

The present value of tax receipts, T, evaluated at the pre-tax rate of interest is given by

$$T = \bar{w}\tau L + \frac{t\bar{r}}{1 + \bar{r}} S \qquad \text{(A.6)}$$

where savings, S, are

$$S = wL - c_1. \qquad \text{(A.7)}$$

Minimizing (A.3) w.r.t. t and τ, subject to (A.6) yields a result which, I believe, is well-known: *The optimum tax rates τ^* and t^* satisfy $t^* = 0$ and*

$\tau^* > 0$, *i.e. capital income is not taxed.* The reason for this outcome in the (logarithmic) model is due (in terms of the Corlett-Hague-Ramsey formulas) to the equality of the cross (compensated) elasticities of consumption in the two periods with leisure. This is equivalent to taxing labor income (subsidizing leisure) alone. Although this result is confined to the logarithmic utility case, it provides a strong *prima facie* case against capital income taxation. Now let us consider the welfare loss due to deviations from the efficient solution.

Suppose, initially, that a comprehensive income tax is in effect (as in the 1986 U.S. tax reform). Let the initial tax rates on labor and capital income be equal at 40 percent: $t = \tau = .4$. The following parameter values correspond to Feldstein (1978):

$$\alpha = .63$$

$$\beta = .07 \qquad \text{(A.8)}$$

$$\gamma = .30$$

These imply a savings rate of 10 percent out of earnings and a marginal propensity to spend on leisure of .3. With a 25-year savings horizon and a pre-tax interest rate of 12 percent per annum, $\bar{r} = 17$. With these parameters, we calculated from (A.6), that $T = .4924$. To keep tax revenues intact, an elimination of the tax on capital income requires raising the tax rate on labor earnings to $\tau = .4205$.

The dead-weight loss of the tax system, L, is defined by

$$L(t,r,u) = E(w,r,u) - E(\bar{w},\bar{r},u) - T(w,r,u). \qquad \text{(A.9)}$$

We can now calculate the gain in the dead-weight loss due to the elimination of the capital income tax, ΔL, keeping tax revenues intact:

$$\Delta L = L(t - \tau - .4,u) - L(t - 0, \tau - .4205, u) = .008535. \quad \text{(A.10)}$$

That is, the tax system without capital income taxation induces a gain of 1.22 percent of initial labor income ($wL = .7$), or about $18 billion in the U.S. economy. This is 1.73 percent of the present value of tax revenue, a significant efficiency gain. However, it turns out that most of the welfare gain is obtained by reducing the capital income tax to 20 percent and a relatively flat welfare function below this level. In fact, 80 percent of the welfare gain could be realized by this reduction. So, when equity considerations are incorporated, it seems reasonable to argue that a 2:1 ratio of labor to capital income taxes strikes an optimal balance between efficiency and equity considerations.

REFERENCES

Feldstein, M. 1978. The welfare cost of capital income taxation. *Journal of Political Economy* 88: 529–51.

Green J. and E. Sheshinski. 1979. Approximating the efficiency gain of tax reforms. *Journal of Public Economics* 11: 179–96.

Pechman, J. 1987. *World tax reform: A progress report.* Washington, D.C.: The Brookings Institution.

———. 1989. Tax reform in an international perspective. Paper presented at a conference at Ben-Gurion University. Mimeo.

Sandmo, A. 1974. A note on the structure of optimal taxation. *American Economic Review* 64: 701–06.

Summers, L. 1983. Capital taxation and accumulation in a life-cycle growth model. *American Economic Review* 71: 533–44.

Tanzi, V. 1987a. The response of other industrial countries to the U.S. tax reform act. *National Tax Journal* (September).

———. 1987b. The tax treatment of interest incomes and expenses in industrial countries: A discussion of recent changes. *National Tax Journal* proceedings.

TAXATION, CORPORATE CAPITAL STRUCTURE, AND FINANCIAL DISTRESS

Mark Gertler
University of Wisconsin and NBER

R. Glenn Hubbard
Columbia University and NBER

EXECUTIVE SUMMARY

Is corporate leverage excessive? Is the tax code distorting corporate capital structure decisions in a way that increases the possibility of an economic crisis owing to "financial instability"?

Answering these kinds of questions first requires some precision in terminology. In this paper, we describe the cases for and against the trend toward high leverage, and evaluate the role played by taxation. While provision of proper incentives to managers may in part underlie the trend to the debt, high leverage may in practice be a blunt way to address the problem, and one which opens up the possibility for undue exposure to the risks of financial distress.

Our story takes as given the kinds of managerial incentive problems deemed important by advocates of leverage. We maintain, however, that when a firm is subject to business cycle risk as well as individual

We are grateful to Rosanne Altshuler, Ben Bernanke, Larry Summers, and participants at the 1989 NBER conference on Tax Policy and the Economy for helpful comments and suggestions.

risk, the best financial arrangement is not simple debt, but rather a contract with mixed debt and equity features. That is, the contract should index the principal obligation to aggregate and/or industry-level economic conditions.

We argue that the tax system encourages corporations to absorb more business-cycle risk than they would otherwise. It does so in two respects: first, it provides a relative subsidy to debt finance; second, it restricts debt for tax purposes from indexing the principal to common disturbances. At a deeper level, the issue hinges on the institutional aspects of debt renegotiation. If renegotiation were costless, then debt implicitly would have the equity features relevant for responding to business cycle risk. However, because of the diffuse ownership pattern of much of the newly issued debt and also because of certain legal restrictions, renegotiation is likely to be a costly activity.

I. INTRODUCTION

Is corporate leverage excessive? Is the tax code distorting corporate capital structure decisions in a way that increases the possibility of an economic crisis owing to "financial instability"?

Answering these kinds of questions first requires some precision in terminology. We refer to a firm as having "excessive leverage" or a "debt overhang problem" when the magnitude of the principal obligation on the debt it is carrying constrains either the amounts it can invest, produce, or employ. In this regard, the business press regularly records fears of the consequences of high leverage.[1] The sharp rise in corporate debt (and debt-service burdens) over the last six years has sparked this concern. The alarm has also spread among circles in the academic community.

On the other hand, the discussions have rarely been precise about how high debt levels could have bad effects on economic activity. Nor has it been made clear why, if high leverage is so dangerous, the private market economy has generated this kind of situation. Finally, there has been an emerging school of thought, led by Jensen (1986, 1988, 1989), which rejects the idea that current leverage is excessive. Instead, it views the current corporate financial situation as simply an efficient market outcome. The efficiency argument rests on the idea that high leverage may provide lenders with a means to restrict indirectly non–value-maximizing behavior by corporate managers.

---

[1] See, for example, Anise C. Wallace, "Time for jitters in the junk bond market," *New York Times*, August 6, 1989.

In this paper, we describe the cases for and against the trend toward high leverage, and evaluate the role played by taxation. While provision of proper incentives to managers may in part underlie the trend to debt, high leverage may in practice be a very blunt way to address the problem, and one which opens up the possibility for undue exposure to the risks of financial distress. We argue that the tax system deserves at least some of the blame for a capital structure that does not optimally shield corporations from the consequences of an economic downturn.

Our story takes as given the existence of the kinds of managerial incentive problems deemed important by the advocates of high leverage. We maintain, however, that when a firm is subject to business-cycle risk as well as individual risk, the best financial arrangement is not simple debt, but rather a contract with mixed debt and equity features. In particular, the arrangement should insulate lenders as much as possible from firm-specific risks but have them share in systemic risks. That is, the contract should index the principal obligation to aggregate and/or industry-level economic conditions. The rough idea is to minimize the impact of a recession on firm net financial positions, as we discuss later in detail.

We proceed to argue that, on the surface, the tax system encourages corporations to absorb more business-cycle risk than they would otherwise. It does so in two respects: First, it provides a relative subsidy to debt finance: second, it restricts debt for tax purposes from indexing the principal to common disturbances. At a deeper level, the issue hinges on the institutional aspects of debt renegotiation. If renegotiation were costless, then debt implicitly would have the equity features relevant for responding to business-cycle risk. However, because of the diffuse ownership pattern of much of the newly issued debt and also because of certain legal restrictions, renegotiation is likely to be a far from costless activity.

The remainder of the paper is organized as follows. Section II summarizes the facts regarding the recent rise in corporate leverage. Section III reviews the main arguments over whether high leverage should be cause for alarm. It describes the benefits of leverage as a corporate control mechanism and the possible costs involved, in terms of raising the possibility of financial distress. This section also addresses the role of taxes in the debate and describes how taxes may distort the capital-structure decision.

Section IV presents some rough evidence regarding the magnitude of the relative tax subsidy to debt. Whether the "new debt" is easy to renegotiate—that is, whether it is effectively equity—is taken up in Section V. Section VI outlines the issues for tax reform using the guiding premise that taxation should not distort corporate capital structure. Finally, Section VII provides some concluding remarks.

II. DEBT AND RECENT CORPORATE FINANCING PATTERNS

The trend to high leverage is relatively new. Over the entire postwar period, equity finance was dominant. For non-financial corporations, retained earnings accounted for roughly 73 percent of funds raised and net new share issues added another 2 percent. Debt provided the balance, divided about equally between private issues (e.g., bank loans and private placements) and public issues (e.g., bonds). Table 1 summarizes this evidence.

Financing patterns altered course during the 1980s. While corporations continue to rely heavily on retained earnings, they have sharply adjusted the composition of external finance. Most notably, there have been substantial equity repurchases, financed mainly with debt (see, e.g., Shoven, 1987). That is, leverage ratios have risen mainly as the product of corporate capital restructurings. Net new equity issues totaled −$131 billion in 1988, as compared to +$25 billion five years earlier.

An important effect of the shift to debt has been a substantial rise in debt-service burdens, and an associated rise in bankruptcies and defaults. Interest payments per dollar of earnings (before interest and taxes) have risen from 16 cents over the postwar period prior to 1970 to 33 cents over the 1970s to an average of 56 cents over the 1980s. Alternatively, interest payments per dollar of cash flow have increased from about 10 cents in the pre-1970 period to about 35 cents over the 1980s. This increase in debt-service burdens (documented in Figure 1) has been accompanied by an increase in corporate bankruptcies and liabilities of business failures over the 1980s. While there has been a cyclical pattern of bankruptcies over the postwar period, bankruptcies have been high (relative to postwar standards) throughout the boom following the 1981–1982 recession (see Figure 2).[2] There is, as well, an impression that larger firms are defaulting on debt obligations (and failing) relative to earlier periods.[3]

---

[2] This increase in bankruptcies raises the question of why bankruptcy costs would be incurred—that is, why renegotiation of financial contracts has not been more effective. We will return to this point repeatedly.

[3] See, for example, Alison Leigh Cowan, "Rescuing business is now a big business," *New York Times*, October 5, 1989.

TABLE 1

*Corporate Financing from Internal and External Sources, 1946–1988
(percentage of total sources)*

Business cycle or year	Retained earnings	Private debt	Corporate bonds	New equity issues
1945:4–1949:4	68.4%	16.2%	12.4%	5.3%
1949:4–1954:2	68.7	6.6	11.1	6.3
1954:2–1958:2	78.4	8.2	10.9	5.4
1958:2–1961:1	79.9	8.0	9.9	4.2
1961:1–1970:4	73.7	12.3	11.1	2.0
1970:4–1975:1	62.0	16.8	11.2	6.5
1975:1–1980:3	74.8	6.5	10.8	2.4
1980:3–1982:4	72.7	19.1	6.2	−0.6
1982:4–1987:4	77.6	12.3	16.0	−12.8
1970	67.3	7.8	21.2	6.1
1971	65.9	4.4	16.6	10.1
1972	68.0	12.0	9.6	8.6
1973	53.3	33.7	5.2	4.5
1974	60.9	17.8	13.4	2.8
1975	82.1	−7.4	17.9	6.5
1976	72.5	3.8	11.7	5.4
1977	74.1	13.0	10.3	1.2
1978	70.7	16.0	8.2	−0.0
1979	77.2	12.4	6.8	−3.1
1980	72.3	7.2	10.0	4.7
1981	68.2	23.7	6.5	−3.3
1982	77.3	14.4	6.0	2.0
1983	74.6	10.0	4.2	6.1
1984	75.6	24.5	10.4	−16.8
1985	81.5	15.3	17.1	−18.8
1986	73.1	10.7	24.8	−16.5
1987	83.0	1.2	23.5	−18.0
1988	85.2	8.7	36.4	−30.3

Source: Board of Governors of the Federal Reserve System, *Flow of Funds Accounts,* various issues; and MacKie-Mason (1989).

As suggested, an important factor underlying the trend to debt has been a dramatic rise in corporate restructurings. Prompting the restructurings have been waves of mergers, acquisitions, leveraged buyouts (LBOs), and defense against LBOs. These restructurings have been particularly significant in raising debt-equity ratios. According to First Boston Corporation (1989, p. 27), the average capital structure of an LBO in 1988 included 87 percent debt (divided among bank debt, 53 percent; coupon debt, 20 percent; and deferred-interest obligations) and only 13 percent equity (divided between common, 10 percent; and preferred, 3

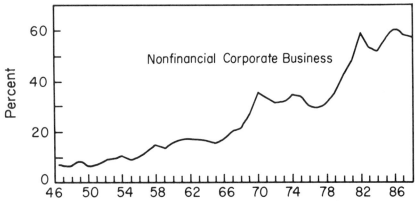

FIGURE 1. *Interest payments relative to corporate earnings
(1946–1988)*

percent). The Office of the Comptroller of the Currency reported that, by the end of 1988, outstanding LBO debt was roughly $150–180 billion. This amounted to about 20 percent of the (book) value of outstanding corporate bonds or over 9 percent of the (book) value of total nonfinancial corporate debt (based on data from the Flow of Funds Accounts). In comparison, from 1978 to 1983, debt emerging from LBO deals was only about $11 billion.

The trend to debt, however, encompasses more than just LBOs. Goldman Sachs has estimated that the equity base of U.S. corporations

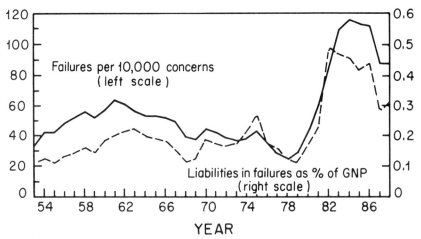

FIGURE 2. *Default and bankruptcy rates (1953–1988)*

shrunk by about $420 billion between 1982 and 1988, and that debt supplanted about three-fourths of this reduction. (*Financial Market Perspectives*, 1988, p. 5).

Another important change in corporate financial policy involved the kind of debt issued. Private debt issues have declined in relative importance. The trend is toward public issues, particularly low grade investments bonds, known popularly as "junk bonds." While junk bonds existed well before the 1980s, widespread use of them has been a relatively sudden event. Seventy percent of outstanding issues (as of the end of 1988) are from the last three years, with 20 percent from 1988 alone (*First Boston Corporation*, 1989, p. 30).

There is no clear consensus on why the junk bond market grew so dramatically. Many observers, though, tend to agree that the development of the secondary market for junk debt (as part of the general trend toward "securitization") was an important factor. This innovation, it is argued, provided junk bonds with the kind of liquidity needed to induce lenders to absorb them on a large scale.[4] An added implication was that it made diffuse ownership of a firm's junk debt possible, and even likely. Thus, along with the general rise in leverage, the 1980s also witnessed a change in the kind of debt issued by corporations—toward debt that involved a more "arms length" relation with bondholders and away from debt, such as bank loans, that permitted a more intimate connection (see Bernanke and Campbell, 1988).

How have junk bonds been faring? After a strong initial performance, total returns on major high-yield funds have fallen significantly in recent years (see Table 2). And for the first half of 1989, the portfolio of high-yield issues reported by *Moody's Bond Survey* (July 17, 1989, p. 5110) had a total return of 5.8 percent versus 11.4 percent for investment-grade bonds—despite the large default premia built into coupon rates.

III. IMPLICATIONS OF INCREASED CORPORATE LEVERAGE, AND THE ROLE OF TAXATION

The case in favor of current trends rests on the idea that the private market is well suited to generate the most efficient kind of corporate

---

[4] The corporate debt "puzzle" is always couched in terms of explaining why current leverage is high. Placed in historical context, an alternative puzzle is why corporate leverage was so low in the 1950s and 1960s (see, for example, Taggart, 1985). The idea that financial innovation was important in the recent development of the junk bond market provides (at least part) of a consistent explanation of both phenomena.

TABLE 2
Total Returns, Sample of High-Yield Funds (Year Ending June 30)

Fund	1989	1988	1987	1986	1985
Dean-Witter High-Yield	4%	2%	11%	23%	23%
Fidelity High Income	9	5	9	24	29
Franklin AGE	8	7	6	18	25.5
Prudential-Bache High Yield	8	6	9	19	25
Putnam High Yield	10	8	9	19.5	23

Note: Returns include price appreciation and reinvestment of capital gains and income dividends.
Source: Lipper Analytical Services.

organization. The case against argues instead that high leverage exposes the economy inordinately to the risks of a severe business downturn; tax considerations rather than pure efficiency considerations, it is held, primarily drive the movement to debt. In this section we first present both sides of the issue and then conclude by discussing the role of taxes.

IIIA. Benefits of Leverage: Debt as an Incentive Mechanism

Those who are sanguine about the rise in leverage typically maintain that debt is desirable because it empowers lenders with an indirect means to monitor the activities of managers. The need for some kind of supervision owes to the separation between ownership and management that is characteristic of the traditional corporate structure. As Berle and Means (1932) originally described, a conflict between ownership and management can emerge if it is difficult for the former to observe and evaluate the activities of the latter. In this kind of environment, management's self interest may not always coincide with efficiently operating the firm (i.e., with maximizing firm value).

Jensen and Meckling (1976) formalized this potential for divergence of interests as an "agency problem." Their work and subsequent by others characterized the efficiency losses ("agency costs") that can arise in this environment. An important insight was that financial contracts could be structured to mitigate the problem. Another was that the managerial stake in the enterprise (the managerial equity) was key: the higher the managerial stake, the closer the gap between managerial interests and value maximization, and hence the lower agency costs. Advocates of increased leverage interpret the recent wave of LBOs in this light. The restructurings improved managerial incentives both by converting the claims of lenders from equity to debt and by concentrating ownership in the hands of management (i.e., by raising the managerial stake).

But why is high leverage the right course? And perhaps more important, why was the movement to high leverage so recent? In general, the efficient financial structure depends on the exact nature of the conflict between ownership and management. For a wide class of situations, it is optimal to make the managers bear as much of the firm-specific risk as possible, the goal being to have managers internalize the gains from maximizing firm value.[5] Debt contracts represent an approximate (sometimes exact) way to implement this kind of solution. By promising lenders a fixed stream of payments, the contract effectively ties managerial rewards closely to the performance of the firm.[6,7]

The idea that debt is a way to properly align managerial incentives is at the core of Jensen's (1986) "free cash flow" theory, perhaps the most prominent explanation for the trend to leverage. The story begins with the idea that managers, if given the leeway, will take advantage of outside lenders' inability to ascertain perfectly whether the firm is investing efficiently. Specifically, managers are inclined to squander cash flow by investing for their own aggrandizement in projects with a negative present value. An arrangement where outside lenders hold debt and managers are the residual claimants is a way to minimize this kind of misuse of cash flow.[8]

The Jensen story also offers some additional insight into why the rise in debt occurred so recently, beyond the conventional story that emphasizes innovation in the secondary market for junk debt. It is observed that (i) high cash flow arises primarily in mature industries, and that (ii) the maturing of American industry in the postwar era began only over the last decade. As a result, the argument goes, the widespread need for corporate restructurings is relatively new (see, for example, Blair and Litan, 1989).

This set of arguments contains some loopholes, however. While

---

[5] Grossman and Hart (1982), for example, show how high debt levels can limit a manager's consumption of prerequisites when firm investment is not easily monitored.

[6] Hall (1988) characterizes these kinds of contracts as "back to the wall," because of the position in which they place management.

[7] One countervailing factor is that the combination of debt finance and limited liability can induce lenders to invest in overly risky projects, if lenders cannot directly monitor investments. In this kind of situation, equity contracts may be optimal.

[8] The value of insiders' stakes for aligning incentives has long been stressed by such practitioners as KKR. Recent accounts have pointed out the role of low insiders' stakes in the failure of the Seaman leveraged buyout. See, for example, Stuart Flack, "See you in bankruptcy court," *Forbes*, October 16, 1989, pp. 77–80.

leveraging the firm may be a way to mitigate the kind of agency problem Jensen describes, it is not immediately obvious that it is the best option. If the objective is to make managers bear the residual risk, then it would seem that other practical means are available. One possibility is to adopt a fixed dividend policy with penalties for management if it fails to meet the payment. If these kinds of alternatives are available,[9] then it appears difficult to explain the debt build-up simply as a response to an emerging agency problem. Tax considerations have likely played a role. If, however, the tax distortion is key, then it is not at all clear that high leverage is the most efficient form of financial organization.

As a matter of theory, high leverage is a very blunt way to align managerial incentives. It works best when most of the variation in cash flow is idiosyncratic to the firm—i.e., when most of the risk is "firm-specific." It works poorly when most of the variation is common across firms, to the extent that debt is costly to renegotiate. The optimal response to the kind of agency problem posed by Jensen insulates lenders as much as possible from the firm-specific risk, but has them share in the common risk. The idea is that managers should be made residual claimants only on the component of profits they can influence—the firm-specific component. For example, managers should not be punished if the firm does poorly during a recession but no worse on average than its competitors. Indeed, to preserve managerial equity—which is valuable for mitigating agency costs—outside lenders should share in the losses to the firm due to an industry-wide or economy-wide recession.

The overall message is that the optimal financial arrangement should link payments to creditors to industry and economy-wide performance (e.g., as would a contract with mixed debt and equity features). Further, because it is desirable to have the outside lenders share in the gains and the losses due to systemic factors, the arrangement is not equivalent to allowing merely for postponement of payment without any adjustment in the present value of the principal obligation. Standard debt contracts do not provide the flexibility needed for sharing of common risks. The

---

[9] Another theoretical possibility is to tie managerial compensation to firm performance, i.e., to use managerial salary rather than capital structure to align incentives. This possibility may be limited in practice, however, by the "business judgment" rule which protects management from liability mistakes of judgment in shareholder challenges in court—as long as management stakes are low (see Gilson, 1986). Yet another alternative in principle is to have the board of directors actively monitor the managers. However, many commentators have lamented the generally weak oversight role provided by outside directors, a role not enhanced by the generally small stake of directors in the firm (see, for example, Shleifer and Vishny, 1988). Similarly, institutional restrictions on banks in the U.S. preclude them from undertaking the kind of extended ongoing monitoring of corporate borrowers that, for example, Japanese banks are free to perform (see Hoshi, Kashyap, and Scharfstein, 1989).

TABLE 3
*Issues of High-Yield Debt (percentage of high-yield debt outstanding,
December 30, 1988)*

First Boston Study		Drexel Burnham Lambert Study	
Containers	4.8%	Heavy Industry	20%
Consumer Manufacturing	8.0	Retailing	14
Chemicals	2.3	Leisure	10
Transportation	7.3	Transportation	8
Media	8.0	Consumer Goods	5
Information and Technology	2.8	Media	11
General Industrial	7.3	Banks and Insurance	7
Food	6.6	High-Tech	5
Energy	7.8	Utilities	4
Consumer Distribution	11.6	Miscellaneous	16
Airlines	2.1		
Acquisition	4.1		
Utilities	5.0		
Metals and Minerals	2.2		
Housing	7.3		
Health Care	2.0		
Gaming and Hotel	5.9		
Finance	3.7		
Entertainment	1.3		

Sources: The categories and calculations are taken from First Boston Corporation (1989, p. 20) and from unpublished Drexel Burnham Lambert data reported in David Zigas and Larry Light, "Don't Put Away the Smelling Salts Yet," *Business Week*, October 2, 1989, pp. 92–93.

advocates of high leverage, however, argue that most debt is easy to renegotiate in practice and, therefore, is implicitly indexed to systemic risks. Whether in fact they are right about renegotiation is perhaps the pivotal question. We will return to this issue frequently.

IIIB. Costs of Leverage: Debt and Financial Stability

A wide spectrum of economists (e.g., Friedman, 1986; and Kaufman, 1986) have voiced concern that corporate restructurings have exposed the economy unduly to the risk of a financial crisis. Ratios of interest obligations to cash flow are at non-recession record highs (see Bernanke and Campbell, 1988). The general fear expressed is that an otherwise normal business downturn could trigger a large wave of bankruptcies, turning the recession into a severe business downturn. This fear is based on the presumption that highly leveraged transactions have occurred in cyclical as well as acyclical industries.

Indeed, a good fraction of the high-yield debt has been issued in manufacturing, a cyclically sensitive industry. Table 3 reports the breakdown of high-yield debt (as of the end of 1988) by industry of issue, using data provided by Drexel Burnham Lambert and First Boston Corporation. Based on the First Boston data, depending on how one allocates the components of the "energy" group between manufacturing and extractive activities, about one-half of the stock of high-yield debt is attributable to manufacturing firms. Similarly, the first five categories in the Drexel enumeration (heavy industry, retailing, leisure, transportation, and consumer goods) which are arguably (relatively) cyclical, account for 57 percent of high-yield debt outstanding.

To put the matter in sharper perspective, Bernanke and Campbell considered the counterfactual experiment of imposing the 1974–1975 business recession on a sample of firms with financial conditions corresponding to 1986 data. The sample was drawn from the Compustat file, and therefore consisted primarily of large firms. The simulations implied that a downturn like 1974–1975 would force more than 10 percent of the sampled firms into bankruptcy.

Any argument that high debt levels are dangerous, however, requires qualification. The institutional structure of the economy is critical. Leverage ratios for non-financial corporations are much higher in West Germany and Japan than in the U.S., for example. The critical difference is that, in these countries, the financial institutions that supply debt typically participate in or monitor closely the activities of the firm. (This is particularly true for Japan—see Hoshi, Kashyap, and Scharfstein, 1989—and for Germany—see Berglof, 1988, and Mayer, 1989.) The close connection between the firm and its major creditor facilitates renegotiation. It thus provides (at least some) of the flexibility needed for adjusting to macroeconomic disturbances. It also serves to directly mitigate the agency problem since the lending institution actively monitors the firm. On the other hand, as Jensen (1988) observes, legal restrictions introduced in the wake of the Depression preclude U.S. financial institutions from directly participating in the activities of nonfinancial corporations. The U.S. system of corporate finance is thus closer to one of diffuse ownership with an arms-length relationship between the firm and its creditors. Further, as implied earlier, the substitution of junk bonds for bank loans in recent years is making this characterization increasingly accurate.[10]

It is also true that the quantity of debt a firm issues must be measured against the quality of its underlying collateral, including the managerial

---

[10] While it is true that banks hold (at least initially) the majority of the senior debt in a highly leveraged restructuring, it is also true that the Comptroller of the Currency has urged them to restrict their holdings to a minimum (see Brancato, 1989).

equity. Perfectly collateralized debt poses no threat, for example. In a less extreme situation, the collateral position is key to evaluating the dangers the firm may face in the event it cannot meet its current interest obligation (but is otherwise solvent for the long term). A firm with a strong position will find it relatively easy to obtain credit to offset the shortfall in its cash flow. One with a weak position is likely to experience the costs of financial distress—suspension of credit flows entailing the need for substantial retrenchment in employment and investment.[11] (For a detailed account of this type of experience, see the description of the Texaco-Pennzoil case in Cutler and Summers, 1988.)

Overall, for the U.S. economy, high debt levels are dangerous to the extent that collateral positions are weak for a significant fraction of corporations and that provisions (either explicit or implicit) do not exist for adjusting the obligations to common risks.[12] The absence of comprehensive indexing permits destabilizing movements in managerial equity. Forcing the corporation to meet fixed interest obligations in a prolonged recession can deplete managerial equity (to the extent managers are the ultimate residual claimants) which in turn can send the company into financial distress. Similarly, non-contingent debt exposes the economy to the risk of unanticipated wealth redistributions that can have adverse effects. For example, the deflation during the Great Depression wiped out a good fraction of the collateral base of non-financial corporations, which had issued liabilities fixed in nominal terms.

There are some corollary factors also suggesting that high debt levels make the economy particularly vulnerable to a recession. One consideration involves the nature of bankruptcy laws in the U.S. These regulations place severe restrictions on the activities of firms in default, thus adding to the real costs of financial distress (again, see Cutler and Summers, 1988). The cumulative effect of a wave of bankruptcies could greatly exacerbate a downturn. And concern for the potential of widespread defaults does not seem misplaced. Asquith, Mullins, and Wolff (1989) have noted that the default rate on junk debt has been rising, despite the economy's having been in a prolonged expansion; specifically, there has been a rise in cumulative default probabilities for the first several years after issue. In addition, the rated quality of the debt has declined.

---

[11] Bernanke and Gertler (forthcoming) emphasize that borrower net worth is likely to be important in the renegotiation process.

[12] The idea that borrower net worth, rather than debt per se, is fundamentally key to financial stability is present in a number of recent studies. See, for example, Bernanke and Gertler (forthcoming); Calomiris and Hubbard (1990); and the review of studies in Gertler and Hubbard (1988).

Two other factors involve external effects. First, a kind of "contagion effect" is possible; the default of a large firm or group of large firms can induce panic among lenders, precipitating a liquidity crisis. An example is the near collapse of commercial paper market in the wake of the Penn Central crisis. News of the impending Penn Central default generated fears of defaults by other firms, prompting a flight of funds out of the commercial paper market (see Brimmer, 1988). Similar effects occurred in the municipal bond market after the WHPPS default; and Hirtle (1988) describes how the LTV default (in July 1986) and the outbreak of the Boesky scandal (in November 1986) had adverse consequences on prices and liquidity of junk bonds.[13] Second, to the extent that there are demand externalities (due, for example, to imperfect competition), the effects of financial distress can spread throughout the economy. In this kind of setting, a downturn in a financially troubled sector can spill over to other sectors (see Cooper and John, 1988, for a discussion of the macroeconomic effects of demand externalities).

IIIC. The Role of Taxes

As we have noted, (in our view) the cause for concern over high leverage rests on the premise that it limits the ability of corporations to optimally share industry and economy-wide risks with outside lenders. To the extent there is a tax incentive encouraging the use of debt relative to equity, it is relevant to consider how the tax system fits into the overall picture.

Ideally, corporations would like to issue securities they could label as "debt" which permitted the legally required principal obligation to vary, perhaps by introducing contingencies on a set of observable indicators. In this way, they could collect the tax benefits from debt finance without sacrificing any flexibility in adjusting to common disturbances. More generally, if allowed the option, firms would like to relabel for tax purposes equity as debt. The spirit of the tax code, at least, precludes this kind of activity. The IRS has generally required that any instrument called debt for tax reasons have a payoff which is "sum certain," (e.g., see the review of cases in Bulow, Summers, and Summers, 1989).[14] Writing a debt contract which either explicitly or implicitly indexes the principal payment to common disturbances violates (at least) the intent of the tax code.

---

[13] Another example, occurring very recently (September 1989), is the response of the high-yield debt market to Campeau's troubles.

[14] In principle, the Secretary of the Treasury can define "debt" for tax purposes, as a result of Congress's addition in 1969 of Section 385 to the Internal Revenue Code. The regulations are administratively complex, however.

It is true that IRS accepts as debt securities which permit interest to be deferred. The recently introduced "payment in kind" bonds are an example. However, these securities meet the "sum certain" requirement because they do not explicitly allow for adjustment of the principal obligation. Thus, at least on the surface, they are not useful instruments for sharing common risks.

There is, accordingly, reason to suspect that the current tax system encourages corporations to adopt a financial structure more exposed to common cyclical risks than would be the case in the absence of any subsidy to debt. In Gertler and Hubbard (1989), we sharpen this point. We study a model of firm investment behavior where the kind of incentive problem deemed important by Jensen is present. Because of certain informational asymmetries, firm insiders (say corporate managers and directors) may try to misallocate investment funds on their own behalf. The financial structure is designed to address the incentive problem. However, the tax system introduces a tradeoff between optimally insulating the firm against business cycle risk and minimizing the expected tax burden.

Under a benchmark tax system that treats all kinds of liabilities symmetrically, the optimal financial arrangement insulates the lenders from as much of the idiosyncratic (firm-specific) risk as possible, but has them share in the aggregate risk. This is in keeping with the arguments presented in Section IIIA. The optimal financial arrangement is interpretable as a mixture of "debt" and "equity." Effectively, equity serves as a buffer to business cycle risks; firms may suspend dividend payments in recessions.[15] This arrangement mitigates the impact of a recession on managerial equity.

Under a tax system that treats debt favorably, firms are induced to issue a smaller fraction of indexed securities (i.e., equity) and thus to absorb more business cycle risk than they would choose in the absence of the distortion. Indeed, if the probability of a recession is sufficiently low, it may be in a firm's interest ex ante to obtain the tax advantage of a high debt-equity ratio at the risk of having a quantity of debt that makes it infeasible to operate in the (ex post) event of a general business downturn. In this situation, because of the large quantity of debt being carried, a recession lowers the net asset position of the firm's insiders to the point where the agency costs are so severe that lenders will no longer

---

[15] It is interesting to observe that, while insignificant over the postwar period, equity issues were an important form of corporate finance prior to the Depression, accounting for more than 15 percent of funds raised during the 1901–1929 period (Taggart, 1985). It is possible that greater cyclical movements (common risks) contributed to the increased reliance on equity finance over that period.

supply credit. The tax system thus encourages the firm to risk the possibility of having a debt-overhang problem in a recession.[16]

We also consider the implications of permitting the principal obligation on debt to be renegotiable. Having (costlessly) renegotiable debt makes debt effectively like equity and thus completely unravels the effect of the tax distortion. The outcome is exactly equivalent to the case of symmetric tax treatment of debt and equity.

Two basic questions emerge directly relevant to public policy. First, how large is the tax subsidy to corporate debt? Second, is debt, particularly the "new" kind of debt, easily renegotiable and thus effectively "equity in drag." If the latter is true then the only public policy question is whether the effective reduction in the corporate cost of capital is desirable. If it is not true, and if the debt subsidy is significant, then it is conceivable that the tax system is encouraging an overly fragile corporate structure.

We address these questions in the next two sections. Section IV discusses the magnitude of the tax subsidy, while Section V takes up the issue of renegotiation.

IV. THE TAX SUBSIDY TO DEBT

In this section we examine the relative tax treatment of debt versus equity. A major point we emphasize is that it is important to distinguish between the incentives provided for using leverage to finance new investments versus using it to repurchase equity. We also try to evaluate recent changes in the tax code in this light.

The relative subsidy to debt is a long-standing feature of the U.S. tax code. It is in part an outcome of the classical system of income taxation under which the incomes to corporations and to the individuals who supply them with funds are taxed separately. Under this kind of system, the effective tax rate on a security depends on its treatment both at the corporate level and the personal level. There are three important "wedges." First, corporations may deduct interest paid to bondholders, but cannot deduct dividends paid to shareholders. Second, individuals must pay taxes on interest as it accrues, as opposed to when it is actually received, but they need to pay taxes on income from stocks (dividends and capital gains) only when it is realized. Third, capital gains have been historically taxed at rates below those on ordinary income.

---

[16] We do not mean to suggest that tax distortions are the only reason financial contracts may not be properly indexed to aggregates. It is, for example, a longstanding puzzle as to why debt contracts are not indexed to the price level. Factors such as the inability to find good indices are probably also important to explaining incomplete indexing.

With respect to choosing between debt and equity to finance new investments, it is relevant to compare the total (corporate and individual) tax burden on each kind of security. The interest deduction at the corporate level, of course, provides a major tax break for using debt. Conversely, the low capital gains rate at the personal level works in favor of equity. In this regard, recent tax changes have had a mixed effect. The 1981 tax act reduced capital gains along with individual tax rates (maintaining the level of the corporate tax rate), while the 1986 act raised them. Specifically, it called for treating realized capital gains as ordinary income (though preserving the advantage of deferral).

For financing new investment, the subsidy to debt finance is

$$t_c + (1 - t_c)t_p^e - t_p^d,$$

where t_c, t_p^e, and t_p^d represent, respectively, effective tax rates on corporate income, and equity and debt income at the individual level. The first two terms represent the taxes paid on returns from an equity-financed investment; the last reflects the tax paid on a return from a debt-financed project (untaxed at the corporate level). The effective tax rate on equity depends on assumptions about the mix of returns between dividends and capital gains as well as the deferral advantage of capital gains.

The effective corporate tax rate will in general be less than the statutory rate because of the tax-loss carryforwards. Altshuler and Auerbach (1990) calculate that during the early 1980s, the effective tax rate was about 32 percent, as opposed to the statutory rate of 46 percent. Gordon and MacKie-Mason (1989) estimate the effective tax rate to be about 29 percent in 1988, as opposed to the statutory rate of 34 percent. Using Poterba's (1989) estimate of t_p^d, they estimate the tax subsidy to debt (implied by the expression above) to be 19.9 percent just prior to the Tax Reform Act of 1986, and 22.4 percent in 1988. Alternatively, using the effective tax rates on interest and equity-return recipients calculated in Table 4, the spread between equity and debt tax rates is larger (30.2 percent).[17] (Both calculations assume that the effective capital gains rate is one-fourth of the statutory rate because of the effects of deferral and stepped-up basis at death; see Feldstein, Dicks Mireaux, and Poterba, 1983.)

The tax considerations involved for deciding to restructure are slightly different from those for financing new investments. Because in this instance leverage is being used to repurchase shares, the net tax cost of

---

[17] In addition, the Deficit Reduction Act of 1984, which eliminated withholding taxes on newly issued corporate bonds, provided incentives for foreigners to increase their holdings of U.S. corporate bonds.

TABLE 4
Effective Tax Rates for Recipients of Debt and Equity Payments

Taxpayer category	1988 Tax rate	Percentage of total	
		Interest receipts (1988)	Equity holdings (1988)
Households (untaxed)	0%	2.8%	[62.0%]
Households (taxed)	28	4.8	
Foreigners	0	12.7	5.4
Commercial Banks	15	5.7	0
Savings and Loans	18	3.0	0
Mutual Savings Banks	6	1.1	0.2
Insurance Companies	20	35.7	5.1
Private Pensions	0	12.7	15.5
State and Local Government Retirement Funds	0	10.9	6.2
Mutual Funds	28	4.4	5.2
Securities Brokers and Dealers	34	1.5	0.9
Weighted-Average		7.3%	19.9%

Sources: Tax rates are taken from Tax Analysts (1986). Interest receipts data are from Summers (1989). Relative ownership of corporate equity in 1988, weighted by the market value of holdings, are obtained from Flow of Funds data published by the Board of Governors of the Federal Reserve System.

issuing debt depends positively on the effective tax on distributions to the existing equity holders, who receive capital gains in process. That is, while a low capital gains rate reduces the subsidy to using debt to finance new capital investment, at the same time it encourages replacing existing equity with debt.

Both corporate and individual tax rates declined after the Tax Reform Act of 1986. In addition, because the statutory capital gains tax rate has been (relatively) high since 1986, it might appear that tax considerations provided little incentive for the mass of corporate restructurings that have occurred since then. On the contrary, even abstracting from deferral advantages, the average effective capital gains tax rate is much lower than the individual income tax rate. This is because capital gains accrue in part to institutional and foreign investors paying lower tax rates. For example, the effective tax rate is zero for pension funds and foreign investors.[18] Moreover, the fraction of equity held by zero-tax investors

[18] The tax rate is "effectively zero" for pension funds, since taxes are paid ultimately by beneficiaries, who are able to defer the obligation, and the advantage of deferral is still quite substantial. Foreign investors also effectively face a zero rate. U.S. capital gains taxes are not levied on foreigners, and withholding taxes on dividends are low for most investors from countries with tax treaties with the United States.

(foreign investors and private and state and local government pension funds) has grown from 12.1 percent in 1970 to 22.1 percent in 1979 to 27.1 percent in 1988. In summary, since interest payments are deductible at the corporate rate, there are still tax incentives underlying the recent switch from debt to equity.

While the tax system encourages the use of leverage, it is unlikely that tax considerations alone are responsible for the current surge in debt. It is hard to pinpoint any recent changes in the tax code that could have promoted a major shift to leverage. A more plausible scenario is that innovations in the junk bond market described earlier (primarily the development of the secondary market) opened up the possibility for corporations to exploit the tax advantage on a much wider scale than was ever possible before.[19]

V. IS DEBT REALLY DEBT?

As we have emphasized throughout, a critical question is whether junk bonds are easily renegotiated in the midst of industry-wide or economy-wide recessions. The claim that junk bonds have the pertinent equity-like features center on five propositions:

  (i) Junk bonds are more closely held than traditional debt, which facilitates renegotiation.
 (ii) The new instruments have fewer restrictions and covenants than traditional private placements, which facilitates trade on a secondary market.
(iii) Original-issue-discount and payment-in-kind obligations permit the issuer to skip cash payments in some periods.
 (iv) Exchange offers of securities can forestall default and bankruptcy in periods of financial distress. Further, incentives are strong to complete these transactions because highly leveraged firms are likely to be valuable ongoing concerns, at least relative to traditional firms in financial distress.
  (v) For reputational considerations, firms like Drexel Burnham Lambert or KKR have a strong incentive to guarantee liquidity in the market.

We address each of these points in turn.

---

[19] Highly leveraged transactions involving unsecured debt have long been common in the financing of small and medium-sized corporations. Traditionally, such transactions consisted of secured debt (60 percent), equity (10 percent), with the balance handled largely through private placements with insurance firms. This market was not large enough to finance large-scale unsecured debt issues necessary to wage war for the control of large corporations (see Perry and Taggart, 1988).

With respect to the first point, the opposite is probably true; holdings of junk bonds are more dispersed than holdings of traditional debt, raising instead of lowering—all other things being equal—the costs of re-negotiation. Over the past decade, non-financial corporations have steadily relied less on bank credit and more on funds obtained from bond markets (e.g., insurance companies, pension funds, and for-eigners). Bank loans provided 44 percent of debt funds raised by non-financial corporations in 1979 and only 21 percent in 1988. Corporate bonds provided just over 25 percent in 1979, and 50 percent in 1988. Bonds used in highly leveraged transactions have in part replaced equity, bank loans, and private placements. While traditional debt was indeed closely held, the same is unlikely to be true for the new debt. The process of securitizing—critical to the growth of the market—makes possible widely diffuse holdings; see Bernanke and Campbell (1988) for related arguments.

Independent studies by Drexel Burnham Lambert and Hirtle (1988) at the Federal Reserve Bank of New York confirm these points. Break-downs of high-yield debt holdings by investor class are reported in Table 5. For example, Hirtle estimates that in 1987, 66 percent of junk bond holdings were in the hands of mutual funds (25 percent), pension funds (10 percent), and insurance companies (31 percent). The balance

TABLE 5
Holdings of High-Yield Debt by Investor Class

Institution or group	Drexel (1986)	New York Fed (1987)	Drexel (1988)
	Holdings as a Percentage of high-yield debt outstanding		
Mutual funds	32%	25%	30%
Insurance companies	30	31	30
Pension funds	10	10	15
Individuals	10	10	5
Savings and Loan Institutions	7	6	7
Foreigners	3		9
Domestic corporations	3	18	3
Securities dealers	1		1
Others	4		0

Sources: Drexel Burnham Lambert data for 1986 are taken from *Report on High Yield Bonds*, General Accounting Office, February 29, 1988. The Federal Reserve Bank of New York data for 1987 are taken from Hirtle (1988). Drexel Burnham Lambert data (as of December 31, 1988) were reported in David Zigas and Larry Light, "Don't Put Away the Smelling Salts Yet," *Business Week*, October 2, 1989, pp. 92–93.

was distributed among individuals (10 percent), savings and loan institutions (6 percent), and other investors (including foreign investors and domestic corporations—18 percent). Further, in addition to complications introduced by dispersion of ownership, "prudent man" rules (under ERISA) governing pension funds and institutions managing pension accounts (see Warshawsky, 1988) may restrict the ability of many institutions to renegotiate.

With respect to the second point, it is no longer true that high-yield debt avoids the restrictions common in traditional private placements. For example, First Boston Corporation (1989, p. 35) reports:

> . . . *the market appears to be coming full circle, back toward the stringent indenture packages of the private placement market. While earlier issues of public high yield securities found that they could trade the liquidity of the public high yield market for the tighter indentures demanded in the private market, many of the more recent issues include covenant packages rivaling those provided in the private market.*

Specifically, the First Boston study notes that as late as 1986, most major deals contained no restrictions on additional debt; by 1987, the major issues reviewed all contained varying degrees of protection against incremental borrowing, thus impeding the ability to renegotiate. This pattern is expected to continue. Other relevant restrictions related to changes in corporate control ("poison puts"), requirements of net worth maintenance, and limitations on certain payments, mergers and consolidations, and asset sales.

The recent issue of senior subordinated notes by Playtex (due December 15, 1988) well illustrates the new restrictions. Though the firm is credited with having a stable market position and consistent operating earnings, Moody's assigned the issue a B2 rating out of concern over interest coverage. The Moody's review indicated a number of covenants relating to changes in control, limitations on debt and dividend payments, and net worth maintenance (*Moody's Bond Survey*, December 19, 1988, pp. 4212–14). The review also expressed concern about the possible effects of leverage on future invstment decisions:

> . . . *A significant risk for Playtex is that it may not have the financial strength to support the marketing and manufacturing programs necessary to build higher sales volume. (p. 4213)*

The third point pertains to the newly introduced debt instruments which permit corporations some flexibility in meeting their interest obligations. There are several kinds. "Original issue discount" bonds defer either all ("zerofix") or part ("split coupon") of the interest payments until maturity. These bonds are growing in popularity: fully 25 percent of new high yield issues in 1988 were original issue discount bonds, and they accounted for 14.4 percent of the stock of high-yield debt and 6 percent of total outstanding corporate debt obligations (First Boston Corporation, 1989, p. 23). "Payment in kind" (PIK) obligations allow the issuer to pay interest in cash or in additional securities (which would be valued at par). These kinds of contracts permit the firm to defer cash payments in periods of distress.

Like equity, these new instruments permit corporations to overcome temporary liquidity problems. However, unlike equity, they do not allow firms to share the risks of systemic disturbances with outside lenders. Both types of instruments, as well as traditional debt, meet the "sum certain" requirement imposed by the IRS. That is, while they permit deferral of interest, they do not allow for costless adjustment of the principal obligation. Thus, they do not permit the kind of indexing necessary to insulate corporations from systemic risks (as described in Section IIIA).

One recent illustration of this point relates to the securities issued in the 1987 purchase of SCI TV by Kohlberg, Kravis, Roberts. The accumulating debt—as cash interest payments are omitted by the financially strapped deal—will grow from $200 million in PIKs in October 1987 to $310 million in October 1990. The result according to one investment manager: "You have a 5-pound bag and 10 pounds of garbage" (see "How KKR Stubbed Its Toe," Business Week, August 7, 1989, p. 56). Other examples have emerged recently, as well.[20]

It is worth emphasizing that the IRS appears determined to prevent firms from simply relabeling equity as debt; in particular, it has taken the sum certain requirement seriously. For example, in 1982, Goldman Sachs attempted to introduce Adjustable Rate Convertible Notes, which allowed for variable payments to bondholders (based on explicit contin-

---

[20] Concern has been expressed that PIK bonds do not adjust the principal obligations. For example:

The wide interest in troubled businesses comes as many companies that loaded up on tax-favored debt capital in recent years are ruing their boundless optimism. Even when a company's income did not justify the debt load, Wall Street's financial engineers often found ways of deferring the out-of-pocket costs.

Known as pay-in-kind securities, increasing-rate notes, or zero-coupon bonds, these exotic inventions cleverly conserve cash in a deal's early years. But the borrower faces a balloon payment on a future day of reckoning. (In Alison Leigh Cowan, "Rescuing businesses is now a big business," New York Times, October 5, 1989.)

TABLE 6
Exchange Offers and Subsequent Defaults (sample of high-yield bonds, by year of issue)

Issue year	Cumulative default percentage (of dollar amount of issues)	Percentage of total issues exchanged ($ amount)	Percentage of total issues exchanged with subsequent default ($ amount)
1977	33.92%	30.95%	49.11%
1978	34.36	20.11	55.17
1979	24.70	4.43	75.00
1980	27.56	17.33	64.62
1981	20.97	29.44	17.81
1982	25.94	7.23	88.89
1983	19.21	13.66	44.51
1984	9.38	4.80	0.00
1985	3.53	3.25	0.00
1986	8.14	1.55	31.25
Totals	10.66%	5.19%	32.81%

Source: Tabulations are based on the study of original-issue high-yield bonds in Asquith, Mullins, and Wolff (1989, Tables, 2, 6, and 7). Cumulative percentages are through December 31, 1988. Defaults refer to bankruptcy filing, formal declaration by the trustee of a bond, or a missed coupon payment. Exchange offers do not include security transactions after default or bankruptcy.

gencies). However, the IRS disallowed the contracts in 1983 for failing to meet the sum certain principle.

Regarding point four, "exchange offers" of securities—the typical mechanism for out-of-bankruptcy renegotiation—are problematic with multiple creditor interests. Such offers are voluntary, raising a "free-rider" problem: debtholders not participating in the exchange of securities may see the market value of their securities subsequently rise, lowering the desire of a given debtholder to participate.

Moreover, historically, completed exchange offers have not provided sufficient breathing room for distressed companies to rebound (First Boston Corporation, 1988, pp. 35–36; 1989, p. 46), and investors have experienced similar losses in distressed exchange offers as in defaults (Asquith, Mullins, and Wolff, 1989). These losses have over the past decade averaged 50.05 percent of principal (First Boston Corporation, 1989, p. 45). Table 6, which uses tabulations from Asquith, Mullins, and Wolff (1989), shows that while exchange offers are not infrequently used, their ability to avoid default is rare.

Another consideration is that the availability of renegotiation under Chapter 11 may provide firms with an attractive alternative to out-of-bankruptcy renegotiation. Under Chapter 11, equity holders and managers have a more significant claim on the enterprise than they would, say, in liquidation. Further, the uniform voting (by creditors) required under Chapter 11 avoids many of the free-rider problems associated with voluntary renegotiation. Out-of-bankruptcy arrangements are not a perfect substitute here, because only Chapter 11 procedures avoid the tendency for bilateral renegotiations. Nor are formal covenants in (publicly issued) bonds. The Trust Indenture Act forbids the inclusion of voting procedures for bondholders to adjust principal and/or interest payments (see Jackson, 1986; or Roe, 1987, for a discussion). Hence, in periods of distress both debtors and creditors may prefer filing for Chapter 11 to voluntary renegotiation; this sentiment is echoed in First Boston Corporation (1989, p. 43).

It is probably true that incentives to complete exchange offers are stronger for highly leveraged firms than for traditional firms, since the value of the underlying assets in the wake of default or bankruptcy is likely to be greater, holding everything else constant. Nonetheless, the weight of (informal) evidence suggests that the frictions owing to the free-rider and institutional considerations mentioned above remain present in the exchange offer process. It is probably also still the case that equity or closely held debt provides better insulation against common risks.

Finally, is it the case that the investment banks and deal makers that have a major stake in the ongoing use of junk bonds will actively intervene to ensure the smooth functioning of the market? Indeed, to date, investment banks such as Drexel Burnham Lambert have played an important role in providing the needed liquidity by actively participating in the secondary market. In our view, these private institutions can perform "lender of last resort" functions when defaults (or near defaults) are relatively isolated incidents. However, it is unlikely that they have the resources to intervene in the midst of a wave of defaults owing to some kind of systemic disturbance. Indeed, the popular perception is that the liquidity of the junk bond market has been drying up as the frequency of defaults has been rising.[21]

VI. THE AGENDA FOR TAX REFORM

We now consider possible reforms which would mitigate the impact of the tax system on corporate capital structure (see also Auerbach, 1989).

One possibility is complete integration of corporate and individual income taxes; this would, of course, eliminate the need to define debt and equity for tax purposes. It would, however, also entail windfalls to

---

[21] See, for example, Anise C. Wallace, "Time for jitters in the junk bond market," *New York Times*, August 6, 1989.

existing equityholders, and eliminate any revenue from investments by foreign shareholders and domestic tax-exempt shareholders. Another possibility is to remove the tax deductibility of interest, which would place debt and equity on a more equal footing. This action, however, would raise the cost of capital to corporations; and it would also confer an advantage on foreign investors in the market for corporate control in the U.S. The latter is true because foreign investors avoid capital gains taxes in the U.S. and may not pay taxes on their U.S. income in their home country (if they are subject to a territorial tax system).

To the extent that corporate-level taxes on capital income are to be maintained, a corporate cash-flow tax provides an alternative way to minimize the differential treatment of debt and equity.[22] Abstracting from the tax treatment of financial institutions, the tax base would be the difference between gross income (receipts less costs of goods sold) and investment expenses. That is, depreciation deductions are replaced by expensing investment, and interest deductions are removed. There is thus no marginal effect of corporate taxation on investment decisions. Nor is there any distinction between returns to existing and new equity, since the tax is effectively on distributions less new equity issues.

The corporate cash-flow tax does not, however, remove all distinctions between debt and equity for tax purposes (see the discussion in Auerbach, 1989). In principle, since the cash-flow tax imposes a zero marginal tax on both debt and equity, the marginal effects of the tax are akin to those of a true income tax in which there are deductions for real returns to both debt and equity. Taking corporate and individual levels of taxation into account, equity returns would have a lower effective tax rate than debt under a cash-flow tax, since interest payments would continue to be taxable for individuals. The transition problems associated with converting to a cash-flow tax are also significant (see the discussion in King, 1986).

VII. CONCLUDING REMARKS

Assessing whether corporate leverage is "too high" requires some kind of metric. We propose one, using an approach that stresses the role of financial contracts in aligning managerial incentives. We argue that, when common as well as idiosyncratic disturbances are important to firm profitability, the optimal financial arrangement involves a mixture of debt and equity. The arrangement is also equivalent to one with debt

---

[22] See, for example, Institute for Fiscal Studies (1978), King (1986), Feldstein (1989), and Hubbard (1989).

that has provisions allowing for adjustment of the principal in response to industry-wide or economy-wide disturbances. The idea is to have outside lenders share the systemic risks in order to insure the firm's financial position, and therefore its creditworthiness, against fluctuations in general business conditions. Our measure of excessive leverage is therefore (roughly speaking) a measure of the degree to which financial contracts are not optimally indexed to cyclical disturbances.

In this regard, distortions contributed by the tax system may be an important factor in creating a situation of excessive leverage. The point is somewhat more subtle than the usual argument that the relative tax subsidy increases the level of debt, thereby increasing the risk of default. The traditional literature, we think, misses the significance of the distinction between idiosyncratic and common risks. As stressed earlier, when only firm-specific risks are important, it is conceivable that pure debt financing is desirable, despite the possibility of costly default and independent of tax considerations. Once common risks are present, however, the tax system introduces a tension. In particular, the authorities who define debt for tax purposes make difficult the kind of indexing provisions desirable for insuring against common risks. This introduces an important tradeoff in the capital structure decision—the benefits from additional debt of the expected tax subsidy versus the costs of having reduced flexibility in adjusting obligations to creditors in the event of an industry-wide or economy-wide recession. We argue further that because junk bonds are costly to renegotiate in practice, it is unlikely that optimal indexing is implicitly present.

We are left with some clear but difficult policy choices. An important problem with the current system is that it seeks to classify particular forms of financial contracts for tax purposes, and thereby interferes with the efficient choice of capital structure. Integrating corporate and individual tax systems or instituting a corporate cash flow tax may be desirable because either avoids the need for this kind of classification, and therefore mitigates the distortion. However, instituting such reforms also requires addressing possible revenue considerations and problems of transition. Nonetheless, discussions of these issues should figure prominently in the debate over corporate leverage.

REFERENCES

Altshuler, Rosanne and Alan J. Auerbach. 1990. The significance of tax law asymmetries: An empirical investigation. *Quarterly Journal of Economics* 105: 61–86 (February).

Asquith, Paul, David W. Mullins, Jr., and Eric D. Wolff. 1989. Original issue high yield bonds: aging analyses of defaults, exchanges, and calls. *Journal of Finance* 44: 923–52 (September).

Auerbach, Alan J. 1989. Debt, equity, and the taxation of corporate cash flows. University of Pennsylvania. Mimeo.

Berglof, Erik. 1988. Capital structure as a mechanism of control: A comparison of financial systems. Discussion paper No. 48, Program in Law and Economics, Harvard Law School (December).

Berle, Adolph and Gardiner Means. 1932. *The Modern Corporation and Private Property*. New York: Macmillan.

Bernanke, Ben and John Y. Campbell. 1988. Is there a corporate debt crisis? *Brookings Papers on Economic Activity*. Washington, D.C., The Brookings Institution, vol. 1: 83–125.

Bernanke, Ben and Mark Gertler. Forthcoming. Financial fragility and economic performance. *Quarterly Journal of Economics* 105: 87–114.

Blair, Margaret M. and Robert E. Litan. 1989. Explaining corporate leverage in the eighties. Washington, D.C., The Brookings Institution. Mimeo.

Brancato, Carolyn K. 1989. Leveraged buyouts and the pot of gold: 1989 update. A Report Prepared for the Use of the Subcommittee on Oversight and Investigations of the Committee on Energy and Commerce, U.S. House of Representatives (July).

Brimmer, Andrew. 1989. Central banking and systemic risks in capital markets. *Journal of Economic Perspectives* 3: 3–16 (Spring).

Bulow, Jeremy I., Lawrence H. Summers, and Victoria P. Summers. 1989. Distinguishing debt and equity in the junk bond era. Harvard University. Mimeo.

Calomiris, Charles W. and R. Glenn Hubbard. 1990. Internal finance, firm heterogeneity, and credit rationing. *Economic Journal* 100 (March).

Cooper, Russell and Andrew John. 1988. Coordinating coordination failures in Keynesian models. *Quarterly Journal of Economics* 103: 441–64 (August).

Cutler, David M. and Lawrence H. Summers. 1988. The costs of conflict resolution and financial distress: evidence from the Texaco-Pennzoil litigation. *Rand Journal of Economics* 19: 157–72 (Summer).

Feldstein, Martin. 1989. Excess debt and unbalanced investment: The case for a cashflow business tax. Testimony before the Committee on Ways and Means, United States House of Representatives, January 31.

Feldstein, Martin, Louis L. D. Dicks-Mireaux, and James M. Poterba. 1983. The effective tax rate and the pre-tax rate of return. *Journal of Public Economics* 21: 129–53.

First Boston Corporation. *High Yield Handbook*. Various issues.

Friedman, Benjamin M. 1986. Increasing indebtedness and financial instability in the United States. In *Debt, Financial Stability and Public Policy*. Federal Reserve Bank of Kansas City.

Friedman, Benjamin M. 1989. Views on the likelihood of financial crisis. In *Reducing the Risk of Economic Crisis*. Martin Feldstein, ed. Chicago: University of Chicago Press, (forthcoming).

Gertler, Mark and R. Glenn Hubbard. 1988. Financial factors in business fluctuations. In *Financial Market Volatility*. Federal Reserve Bank of Kansas City.

Gertler, Mark and R. Glenn Hubbard. 1989. Corporate taxation, capital structure, and aggregate fluctuations. Columbia University. Mimeo.

Gertner, Robert and David Scharfstein. 1989. The effects of reorganization law on investment efficiency. MIT Mimeo. May.

Gilson, Ronald J. 1986. *The Law and Finance of Corporate Acquisitions*. Mineola, New York: The Foundation Press.

Gordon, Roger H. and Jeffrey K. MacKie-Mason. 1989. Effects of the Tax Reform Act of 1986 on corporate financial policy and organization form. University of Michigan. Mimeo. September.

Grossman, Sanford and Oliver Hart, 1982. Corporate financial structure and managerial incentives. In *The Economics of Information and Uncertainty*. John McCall, ed. Chicago: University of Chicago Press.

Hall, Robert E. 1988. Financial factors in business fluctuations: commentary. In *Financial Market Volatility*. Federal Reserve Bank of Kansas City, 73–78.

Hoshi, Takeo, Anil Kashyap, and David Scharfstein, 1989. Bank monitoring and investment: Evidence from the changing structure of Japanese corporate banking relationships. In *Asymmetric Information, Corporate Finance, and Investment*. R.G. Hubbard, ed. Chicago: University of Chicago Press (forthcoming).

Hubbard, R. Glenn. 1989. Tax corporate cash flow, not income. *The Wall Street Journal*, February 16.

Institute for Fiscal Studies. 1978.*The Structure and Reform of Direct Taxation*: London: Allen and Unwin.

Jackson, Thomas H. 1986. *The Logic and Limits of Bankruptcy Law*. Cambridge: Harvard University Press.

Jensen, Michael C. 1986. Agency costs of free cash flow, corporate finance, and takeovers. *American Economic Review* 76: 323–29 (May).

Jensen, Michael C. 1988. Takeovers: their causes and consequences. *Journal of Economic Perspectives* 2: 21–48 (Winter).

Jensen, Michael C. 1989. Active investors, LBOs, and the privatization of bankruptcy. *Journal of Applied Corporate Finance* 2: 35–44 (Spring).

Jensen, Michael C. and William Meckling. 1976. Theory of the firm: managerial behavior, agency costs, and ownership structure. *Journal of Financial Economics* 1: 305–60 (October).

Kaufman, Henry. 1986. Debt: the threat to economic and financial stability. In *Debt, Financial Stability, and Public Policy*. Federal Reserve Bank of Kansas City.

MacKie-Mason, Jeffrey K. 1989. Do firms care who provides their financing? In *Asymmetric Information, Corporate Finance, and Investment*. R.G. Hubbard, ed. Chicago: University of Chicago Press (forthcoming).

Mayer, Colin. 1989. Financial systems, corporate finance and economic development. In *Asymmetric Information, Corporate Finance, and Investment*. R.G. Hubbard, ed. Chicago: University of Chicago Press (forthcoming).

Myers, Stewart C. 1977. Determinants of corporate borrowing. *Journal of Financial Economics* 5: 146–75 (November).

Perry, Kevin and Robert Taggart. 1988. The growing role of junk bonds in corporate finance. *Continental Bank Journal of Applied Corporate Finance* 1: 37–45 (Spring).

Poterba, James M. 1989. Tax reform and the market for tax-exempt debt. Working Paper No. 2900. National Bureau of Economic Research.

Roe, Mark. 1987. The voting prohibition in bond workouts. *The Yale Law Journal* 97: 232–79.

Shleifer, Andrei and Robert Vishny. 1988. Value maximization and the acquisition process. *Journal of Economic Perspectives* 2: 7–20 (Winter).

Shoven, John B. 1987. The tax consequences of share repurchases and other non-dividend cash payments to equity owners. In *Tax Policy and the Economy*, vol. 1, Lawrence H. Summers, ed. Cambridge: MIT Press.

Summers, Lawrence H. 1989. Taxation and corporate debt. Testimony before the Committee on Finance, United States Senate, January 25.

Taggart, Robert A. 1985. Secular patterns in the financing of U.S. corporations. In *Corporate Capital Structures in the United States*. Benjamin M. Friedman, ed. Chicago: University of Chicago Press.

Tax Analysts. *Quantifying the Impact of the Tax Reform Act of 1986 on Effective Corporate Tax Rates.*

Warshawsky, Mark. 1988. Pension plans: funding, assets, and regulatory environment. *Federal Reserve Bulletin* (November).

DEMOGRAPHICS, FISCAL POLICY, AND U.S. SAVING IN THE 1980S AND BEYOND

Alan J. Auerbach
University of Pennsylvania and NBER

Laurence J. Kotlikoff
Boston University and NBER

Like virtually all developed economies, the United States is projected to experience a dramatic demographic transition over the next 50 years. By 2040 31 percent of the U.S. population will be 55 and older compared to 21 percent today (see Table 1). Most of this aging will occur among the older old with the fraction of the population over 65 predicted to almost double. While the burden on the working population of supporting dependents will be reduced somewhat due to the lower projected ratio of children to middle-aged adults, the overall dependency ratio (the ratio of those under 18 plus those 65 and older to those 18 and 64) will rise from its value of .616 in the 1980s to .730 in the 2040s.

A higher dependency ratio leads to more consumption relative to output and a lower saving rate. For the U.S., which has been experiencing a remarkably low rate of saving in the 1980s, the prospect of even lower saving rates in the future is daunting indeed. Since saving represents the increase in capital, the saving decline would spell a decline in

We thank Jinyong Cai, Jagadeesh Gokhale, and Manjula Singh for helpful comments and excellent research assistance. We are also very grateful to Alice Wade of the Social Security Administration for providing population projections and the National Institute of Aging and the National Bureau of Economic Research for providing research support.

TABLE 1
Population Age Distributions for the U.S. by Decade

Age group	1950s	1960s	1970s	1980s	1990s	2000s
0–17	.329	.356	.318	.268	.256	.239
18–24	.109	.114	.143	.140	.111	.110
25–34	.133	.109	.125	.156	.146	.120
35–54	.256	.240	.220	.228	.277	.299
55–64	.090	.088	.092	.092	.083	.103
65 plus	.084	.093	.102	.116	.126	.129

Age group	2010s	2020s	2030s	2040s
0–17	.222	.216	.210	.207
18–24	.106	.097	.097	.096
25–34	.123	.117	.111	.113
35–54	.269	.253	.255	.249
55–64	.132	.128	.113	.120
65 plus	.148	.188	.214	.215

the capital-labor ratio were it not for the fact that the demographic transition also involves slower growth in the nation's labor supply. On balance, capital-labor ratios are likely to rise in the developed economies (see, for example, Auerbach, et al., 1989). Higher capital-labor ratios will alter factor prices by raising real wages and lowering the real return to capital. These changes in factor prices will redound to the benefit of workers in the first half of the next century, but to the detriment of contemporaneous retirees who will receive lower returns on their savings. This intergenerational "incidence" of the demographic transition will mitigate, somewhat, the increased fiscal burden expected to fall on future workers.

The size of the burden on future workers will depend, of course, on the fiscal policy response to the demographic transition. With the very significant 1983 Social Security Amendments (which raised the Social Security retirement age and made Social Security benefits taxable under the income tax) the retirement\disability portion of the Social Security payroll tax appears to be in financial balance in the long run. In contrast, the Medicare component of Social Security is slated to require additional funds or benefit cuts around the turn of the century. These projections reflect the Social Security Administration's (SSA's) intermediate actuarial assumptions. According to the SSA's pessimistic projections, the combined retirement\disability and Medicare programs will be in significant financial trouble by 2020. Even the pessimistic projections assume the accumulation of a substantial Social Security trust fund over the next two decades which will help pay for the retirement benefits of the baby boom generation. If the federal government responds to the near-term Social Security receipts by reducing payroll or other taxes, as is now being done implicitly by including Social Security surpluses in meeting the Gramm-Rudman-Hollings deficit targets, the result will be even larger burdens on the children and grandchildren of the baby boomers.

A related concern about fiscal policy has to do with the growing political power of the elderly. While the elderly, defined here as those 55 and older, currently represent one-fifth of the voting age population, they will represent almost a third of potential voters by 2020. In exercising their increased political power, the elderly may seek additional transfers from the government, which ultimately means from young and future generations, or, what amounts to the same thing, the elderly may seek to reduce their tax obligations to the government. A recent example of this process is the dispute over the Medicare surcharge introduced in 1988 (and repealed in 1989) to pay for the catastrophic health care for the elderly.

Since the elderly, as a group, appear to consume a greater fraction of their wealth annually than the young (Abel, Bernheim, and Kotlikoff, 1989) and, certainly, than unborn generations, additional redistribution toward the elderly will mean additional downward pressure on the U.S. saving rate.

This paper focuses on U.S. saving, demographics, and fiscal policy. It addresses the following questions: first, what has been the pattern of postwar U.S. saving rates—specifically, have saving rates declined in the 1980s and by how much? Second, is the apparent drop in the saving rate dependent on how one defines saving? Third, is demographic change responsible for low U.S. saving in the 1980s? If not, what is? Fourth, how are the projected demographic changes over the next 50 years likely to affect saving rates during this period? Fifth, since the time path of saving rates is critical to the time path of current account deficits in an open economy such as the U.S., how will the demographic transition influence future current accounts? Sixth, how do fiscal policy and demographics interact in affecting saving, i.e., how much more detrimental to saving are policies that redistribute toward the elderly if they occur at a time when the population is quite aged?

The next section of this paper describes recent U.S. saving behavior, pointing out that saving has declined in the 1980s according to a variety of alternative measures of saving and income. Section II uses data from the Consumer Expenditure Surveys of the 1980s to consider how demographics may affect saving rates. The analysis uses the age-consumption, age-earnings, and age-capital income profiles observed in these data and asks how saving rates in the past as well as the future would have looked and would look were these profiles time-invariant. This experiment asks, then, how saving rates respond to changes in the age distribution of the population holding all else constant. The analysis leads to a prediction of higher saving rates in the 1990s, but steadily declining rates of saving thereafter. The results also suggest, rather strongly, that demographics *cannot* explain the low rate of U.S. saving in the 1990s, nor, indeed, the postwar pattern of U.S. saving.

Section III considers the interaction of future fiscal policies and demographics with respect to future U.S. saving. We show that changes in the age distribution of the population are likely to have only minor effects on government consumption and U.S. saving given the current pattern of government consumption expenditures by age. In contrast, intergenerational shifts in the burden of fiscal policy may shift the age-distribution of private consumption and have important effects on future saving rates, with these effects accentuated by the aging of the population.

Section IV turns to the question of future current account deficits. The analysis here is partial equilibrium in nature in the sense that the world interest rate is taken as given. Still, the results seem interesting. Our calculations lead to the prediction of positive, but declining current accounts (surpluses) over the next 50 years. Section V returns to the question of saving in the 1980s, discussing other explanations for its decline. Section VI summarizes and concludes the paper by pointing out that our approach toward understanding the effects of demographic change on saving is only one of many that could and should be considered.

I. RECENT SAVING BEHAVIOR IN THE UNITED STATES

A meaningful discussion of the level and determinants of the U.S. saving rate requires care in defining saving. In general terms, saving equals income less consumption, but one must resolve various ambiguities concerning the measurement of income and consumption. There are a number of different measures of aggregate saving, some of which bear little relationship to an economist's notion of saving. In this section of the paper, we review and evaluate the alternative measures commonly used and discuss their performance during the past decade. This will provide a clearer picture of the recent decline in the U.S. saving rate. Our analysis indicates that while the rate of saving may depend heavily on one's definition, measurement issues alone do not alter the conclusion that the rate of U.S. saving declined significantly during the 1980s.

Before discussing these findings, it will be useful to review some national income definitions and accounting identities. Because we are interested in net additions to national wealth, we begin with the aggregate income measure that excludes depreciation from Gross National Product (*GNP*), the Net National Product (*NNP*). Other income measures include Disposable National Income (*DNI*), equal to *NNP* plus government transfers (*R*) less taxes paid (*T*):

$$DNI = NNP - T + R \qquad (1)$$

and Disposable Personal Income (*DPI*), equal to disposable national income less undistributed corporate profits, usually referred to as business saving:

$$DPI = DNI - BS. \qquad (2)$$

Each of these measures of income, *NNP*, *DNI*, and *DPI*, is commonly used as a base for measuring saving. (Note that, according to government accounting procedure, transfers *R* include interest payments on the national debt to U.S. households and businesses.)

In addition to different measures of income, alternative saving measures are based on different notions of consumption. The most basic measure is household consumer expenditures from the national income accounts, *C*. The broader measure would include government expenditures, *G*. To correct for the fact that some household expenditures on consumer durables really represent investment, and that, likewise, some government spending should really be categorized as investment (there is no official government capital account) one can adjust these measures by subtracting the investment component of current expenditures, *CI*, and adding back in the imputed rent on such expenditures, *GIR*.

$$CC = C - CI + CIR \qquad (3)$$

$$GC = G - GI + GIR. \qquad (4)$$

Making these corrections also alters the corresponding measure of aggregate income. Aggregate investment spending rises by *CI* + *GI*, exceeding the decline in measured consumption by *CIR* + *GIR*. To

TABLE 2
Postwar Saving Rates in the United States

Years	Personal (HSR)	Private (PSR)	National (NSR)	National, corrected
1950–1959	6.8	10.4	9.2	13.3
1960–1969	6.7	11.2	8.9	13.0
1970–1979	8.0	11.1	8.5	11.8
1980	7.1	8.9	6.8	8.4
1981	7.5	9.3	7.4	8.9
1982	6.8	7.6	3.2	4.7
1983	5.4	7.8	3.3	5.5
1984	6.1	9.3	5.7	8.6
1985	4.4	7.8	3.6	7.1
1986	4.0	7.2	2.8	na
1987	3.2	5.6	2.7	na
1988	4.2	6.3	3.8	na

na: not available

Sources: 1950–1987: Economic Report of the President, 1989; 1988: Survey of Current Business, June 1989

Imputed rent on an asset is calculated as annual depreciation plus 3 percent times the stock of the asset. Annual depreciation of consumer durables and government non-military tangible assets as well as the stocks of consumer durables and government tangible assets are reported in the U.S. Dept. of Commerce's *Fixed Reproducible Tangible Wealth in the United States, 1925–1985.*

maintain the consistency of the national income identity that net national product equals consumption plus net investment plus government spending plus net exports, one must therefore add the imputed rent on consumer and government capital to net national product:[1]

$$NNPC = NNP + CIR + GIR. \tag{5}$$

With these definitions of income and consumption, we now discuss recent trends in U.S. saving behavior. Table 2 provides annual values of several different measures of saving over the past decade. The first

[1] The corrected net national product measure adjusts the National Income Accounts measure of net national product by 1) adding the imputed rent on consumer durables and government tangible assets, excluding military equipment (expenditure on which is treated as current consumption) and 2) subtracting the depreciation on the stock of consumer durables and government tangible assets (excluding military equipment). Corrected private consumption measure equals private consumption expenditure on goods and services plus the imputed rent on consumer durables. Corrected government consumption equals the National Income Account measure of government consumption less government expenditures on (non-military) equipment and structures, plus the imputed rent on government equipment (non-military) and structures.

column presents the personal saving rate, perhaps the most commonly cited measure of saving. This is the fraction of disposable income that households save.

$$HSR = (DPI - C)/DPI = HS/DPI. \qquad (6)$$

It averaged 6.8 percent during the 1950s, 6.7 percent during the 1960s, and 8.0 percent in the 1970s. Annual values for the period 1980–1982 fall among these averages. Since then the personal saving rate has fallen considerably, averaging less than 4 percent during the period 1985–1988. While the personal saving rate has risen slightly in 1988, it is still well below the averages of previous decades.

Though popular, the personal saving rate has several shortcomings that raise questions about its usefulness. First, a significant fraction of saving has traditionally been done by business, so looking only at personal saving may provide a misleading picture of the overall saving rate. Second, empirical research (David and Scadding, 1974 and, more recently, Auerbach and Hassett, 1989) has suggested that personal and business saving are closely related, that personal saving decisions respond to those of business and cannot be understood in isolation. Third, the accounting conventions used to define personal income and saving are necessarily arbitrary. For example, though they are essentially equivalent transactions, the payment of dividends reduces business saving and increases personal disposable income and saving, while a redemption of corporate shares does neither. A rise in nominal interest payments by corporations to households caused by an increase in the inflation rate also increases measured household income and saving at the expense of corporate saving, without anything real having happened. Since the 1980s has been a period during which the inflation rate and the mix of dividends and share repurchases among corporate distributions has changed significantly, these accounting conventions may distort one's inferences about recent saving.

Moving to the private saving measure, which includes household and business saving, eliminates these problems. Such a measure is given in the second column of Table 2. This private saving rate,

$$PSR = (DPI + BS - C)/(DPI + BS) = (DNI - C)/DNI = PS/DNI \qquad (7)$$
$$= (HS + BS)/DNI = (NNP - T + R - C)/(NNP - T + R)$$

is essentially equal to the fraction of private sector disposal income not consumed by households. It is higher than the personal saving rate but shows the same drop in the 1980s. The private saving rate is more indicative of the rate of household wealth accumulation than the personal saving rate because households own businesses. If businesses accumulate assets, these assets belong to households, and should therefore be included in our measure of saving. A similar argument may be made with respect to government saving. Accumulations of assets by the government increase national wealth, just as private accumulations do. While the rights to such accumulations may be less easily assigned to any one group of households, they certainly represent additions to the wealth of the population (current and future) as a whole, since the population controls (owns) the government. Like the personal-private saving distinction, the distinction between government and private saving is, according to much of economic theory, entirely arbitrary. For example, a decision by the government to call Social Security contributions "loans to the government," rather than "taxes," and Social Security benefits, "repayment of these loans," rather than "government transfer payments" would dramatically alter the reported values of private and government saving, but should not alter the sum of government plus private saving. As before, this point argues for a broader measure of saving including public as well as private accumulations. Such a measure, defined by

$$NSR = (DNI + T - R - C - G)/(DNI + T - R)$$

$$= (NNP - C - G)/NNP$$

(8)

is given in the third column of Table 2. This national saving rate equals the fraction of net national product not devoted either to consumption or government spending.

Like the personal and private saving rates, the national saving rate declined during the 1980s. However, the drop was more precipitous, with the national saving rate averaging just 3.2 percent during the period 1985–1988.

A final measure of national saving incorporates the corrections for household and government investment discussed above:

$$NSRC = (NNPC - CC - GC)/NNPC = NSC/NNPC$$ (9)

This measure, given in the fourth column of Table 2, in general shows much higher levels of national saving than the uncorrected measure in column 3. This indicates that a considerable amount of national saving occurs through the usually ignored channels of household and government purchases of capital goods. However, the correction further accentuates the decline in national saving in the 1980s. While the average uncorrected national saving rate in the 1980s was 3.5 percentage points lower than in the 1970s, the average corrected measure fell by 4.6 percentage points.

In summary, the measures of the U.S. saving rate presented in this section vary considerably in their estimates of the fraction of income saved in the 1980s. However, all measures of the saving rate indicate a very clear decline during the 1980s.

II. DEMOGRAPHICS AND SAVING RATES

Several researchers have remarked about the relative stability of the shape of U.S. cross section age-consumption and age-earnings profiles in the postwar period (Kotlikoff and Summers, 1981, and Carroll and Summers, 1989). The stability of these profiles suggests asking what saving rates would be in the future if these profiles retain their shapes and current levels; i.e., suppose consumption, earnings, and capital income at each age as well as the age-pattern of government consumption expenditure stayed the same, how would saving rates evolve over time as the age distribution of the population changes? The methodology underlying this exercise is described in detail in the Appendix. The population data used in this analysis come from the Social Security Administration and represent historical figures and projections based on intermediate assumptions. The relative age-sex consumption, earnings, and capital income profiles were derived from data based on the 1980 through 1985 Consumer Expenditure Surveys (CES) of the U.S. Bureau of Labor Statistics.[2] The method used to determine the age-pattern of

---

[2] For the consumption profile, the procedure began with an allocation of total consumption reported by CES households to members within the household. Some of the household consumption expenditures, such as a child's clothing, could be allocated more accurately than general expenditures, such as food. Such general expenditures were divided evenly among adults (individuals over 18) and children, but under the assumption that each child's consumption of general expenditures is one-third of that of an adult. The resulting data, which consisted of individual consumptions indexed by age and sex, were next used to form the weighted (based on CES population weights) average value of average consumption by age and sex for the quarter in question. These values were then divided by the corresponding quarter's weighted average of consumption of 40-year-old males. The resulting relative consumptions indexed by age, sex, and quarter were then regressed against fifth-order polynomials interacted with sex dummies. The predicted values for this regression provide the values of the $R^c_{a,m,t}$'s and the $R^c_{a,f,t}$'s. The method of deriving the values of the $R^e_{a,m,t}$'s and the $R^e_{a,f,t}$'s is essentially the same except for the fact that reported earnings are annual and there is no problem of allocating earnings to the correct individual. The same general method is also used to derive the $R^k_{a,m,t}$'s and the $R^k_{a,f,t}$'s profiles. However, rather than using reported capital income which is likely to

TABLE 3

The Effect of Demographics on Saving Rates for Fixed Age-Earnings, Age-Consumption, and Age-Government Consumption Profiles

Decade	Predicted saving rates Base year					Actual U.S. saving rates
	1987	1980	1970	1960	1950	
1950–1959	.013	.090	.128	.110	.117	.092
1960–1969	− .041	.042	.082	.064	.074	.089
1970–1979	− .037	.045	.084	.066	.075	.085
1980–1989	.014	.090	.128	.109	.115	.044*
1990–1999	.053	.125	.160	.142	.147	
2000–2009	.068	.139	.173	.156	.161	
2010–2019	.065	.137	.170	.154	.160	
2020–2029	.045	.119	.151	.136	.146	
2030–2039	.030	.105	.136	.122	.133	
2040–2049	.026	.101	.132	.118	.129	

* This average is over the period 1980–1988.

government consumption expenditure is described in Auerbach, et al. (1989).

Table 3 reports the average decade saving rates that are predicted based on equation (1) for five different base years: 1950, 1960, 1970, 1980, and 1987. There are several striking features of this table. First, for each of the base years the saving rate is predicted to rise over the course of the next three decades and then decline somewhat over the following three decades. Taking 1987 as the base year, the predicted saving rate in the 1980s is 1.4 percent; it is 5.3 percent in the 1990s, rises to 6.5 percent in the period 2010–2019, and then declines to 2.6 percent in the 2040s. The predicted pattern of saving rates reflects the aging of the population coupled with the fact that the difference between average (over males and females) earnings and average consumption at a given age is, in the case of the 1987 base year, negative for ages 20 and below, positive between ages 20 and 58, and negative after age 58. Figure 1 plots the difference between average age-earnings and age-consumption profiles for the base year 1980. The corresponding figure for other base years is quite similar. Figure 1 can be compared with Figure 2 which plots the age distribution of the population for a select set of years.

greatly understate true capital income, we used the CES asset data to form annual observations of weighted average net worth by age and sex. Net worth is the sum of financial assets, such as stocks, bonds, and checking accounts, and real estate, less mortgages and other liabilities. A description of the net worth calculation is provided in Abel, Bernheim, and Kotlikoff (1989).

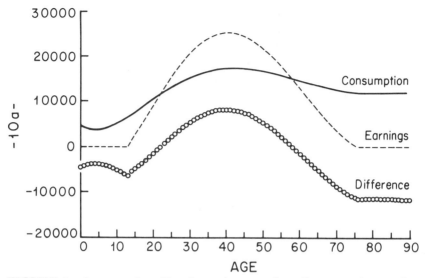

FIGURE 1. *Average Age–Earnings, Average Age–Consumption, and the Difference*

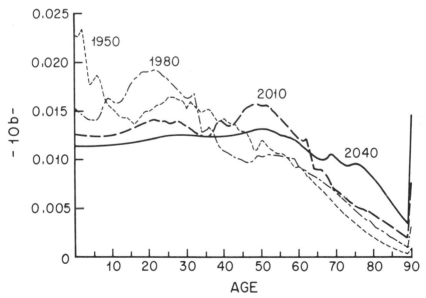

FIGURE 2. *Share of Total Population at Particular Age*

A second important feature of the table is that the predicted pattern of saving rates in this decade and the previous three decades do not match up very well with the observed pattern of saving rates. From demographics alone one would have predicted high saving rates in the 1950s and 1980s and low saving rates in the 1960s and 1970s. Clearly, much more than demographics appears to be at play in the data. Further research is needed to determine the precise explanation for the failure of Table 2's predicted time pattern of saving rates to match the actual postwar pattern.[3] Still, the table suggests that demographic change can, itself, have very powerful effects on national saving rates.

III. FUTURE SAVING RATES AND THE INTERACTION OF FISCAL POLICY AND DEMOGRAPHICS

The saving rate simulations of Table 3 implicitly hold constant fiscal policy. This section considers how possible changes in government consumption and intergenerational policy affect the predicted saving rates. We consider first the question of government consumption spending, holding fixed the age-consumption, age-earnings, and age-capital income profiles. With these household profiles held fixed, Table 4 asks how the predicted national saving rates would be affected by a change in our assumption about the response of government spending to demographic shifts.

The calculations reported in Table 3 assumed a constant age-specific pattern of government consumption spending. Table 4 presents simulations based on the alternative assumption that government consumption per capita remains fixed through time at the various base year values. That is, we hold constant government spending per capita rather than government spending per member of particular age groups. Under our previous assumption, increases in per capita spending would automatically have been predicted by a shift (from the base year) in the share of the population accounted for by those groups, such as the elderly, who individually receive substantial levels of government services.

A comparison of Tables 3 and 4 shows that assuming fixed per capita government consumption expenditures leads to only slightly lower predicted saving rates over the next 50 years. At least one reason for this is that the increases in per capita government spending anticipated in the

---

[3] A better fit does not arise from assuming that the ratio of child to adult consumption of general consumption expenditures (those that cannot be identified in the CES data as child- or adult-specific) is one-half rather than one-third.

TABLE 4
*The Effect of Demographics on Saving Rates for Fixed Age-Earnings
and Age-Consumption Profiles and Fixed Per Capita
Government Consumption*

	Predicted saving rates Base year					Actual U.S. saving rates
Decade	1987	1980	1970	1960	1950	
1950–1959	.016	.088	.123	.107	.118	.092
1960–1969	−.031	.045	.081	.066	.080	.089
1970–1979	−.029	.042	.083	.068	.081	.085
1980–1989	.016	.088	.123	.107	.117	.044*
1990–1999	.050	.120	.154	.138	.147	
2000–2009	.063	.132	.165	.151	.161	
2010–2019	.059	.130	.162	.149	.150	
2020–2029	.043	.115	.147	.136	.140	
2030–2039	.030	.130	.136	.124	.140	
2040–2049	.025	.099	.131	.120	.136	

* This average is over the period 1980–1988.

simulations reported in Table 3 are not that significant. Although the elderly receive a disproportionate share of government spending, so do the young (primarily on education). As the population ages, the decline in spending on the young partially offsets the increase in spending on the old in the simulations reported in Table 3.

Table 5 considers a related, but more extreme policy change. Suppose that all funds spent on age-specific government items in the base year had been directed toward the elderly, and that the level of this spending per elderly person were kept fixed even as the fraction of elderly in the population increased over time. This experiment reflects the potential shift in government spending that would result were the elderly able to redirect all age-specific spending toward themselves and maintain such spending levels over time; it surely represents the largest plausible estimate of the possible impact of population aging on government spending.

Since the predicted saving rates in Table 5 incorporate this very strong assumption, comparing Table 5 with Table 3 indicates the maximum saving effect likely to arise if the elderly, because of increased political influence, were able to redirect all of the age-related government consumption expenditure (which excludes defense, etc.) to spending on themselves. Indeed, such an outcome would have a significant impact on national saving. As the population ages, a large increase in govern-

TABLE 5
The Effect of Demographics on Saving Rates When All Age-Related Government Consumption Expenditures Are All Spent on the Elderly

| Decade | Predicted saving rates Base year | | | | | Actual U.S. saving rates |
	1987	1980	1970	1960	1950	
1950–1959	.046	.110	.135	.113	.114	.092
1960–1969	− .007	.060	.084	.063	.068	.089
1970–1979	− .013	.054	.077	.056	.062	.085
1980–1989	.019	.083	.105	.083	.089	.044*
1990–1999	.045	.107	.127	.106	.112	
2000–2009	.056	.118	.137	.117	.125	
2010–2019	.037	.101	.117	.099	.111	
2020–2029	− .012	.055	.065	.049	.070	
2030–2039	− .047	.022	.029	.012	.040	
2040–2049	− .053	.016	.022	.007	.034	

* This average is over the period 1980–1988.

ment spending per capita would occur under the assumptions used to produce Table 5. This leads to a significant fall in predicted saving rates after the turn of the century. For example, using 1980 as the base year, we find that the predicted national saving rate for the decade beginning in 2020 falls from 11.9 percent in Table 3 to 5.5 percent in Table 5.

In addition to changes in government consumption, a second important dimension of fiscal policy that can affect saving is the government's intergenerational policy, by which we mean the extent to which the government places the burden of paying for its consumption on different age groups. If the growing political power of the elderly leads to reduced taxes on the elderly and more transfers to them, this should have the effect of rotating the age-consumption profile toward more consumption by the elderly and less consumption by the young. Table 6 considers the effects of such a rotation on the predicted saving rates. Specifically, we adjust the benchmark profile of consumption by age (keeping base year consumption constant) by increasing the relative consumption of those over 65 relative by 5 percent and reducing the relative consumption of those under age 45 by 5 percent. Roughly speaking, one may view this as simulating the effect of cutting taxes on the elderly by 5 percent of income and raising taxes on the young by 5 percent of income.

As a comparison of Tables 3 and 6 indicates, altering the age-consumption profile in this manner leads to somewhat higher predicted

TABLE 6
The Effect of Demographics on Saving Rates When the
Age-Consumption Profile is Rotated in Favor of the Elderly

Decade	Predicted saving rates Base year					Actual U.S. saving rates
	1987	1980	1970	1960	1950	
1950–1959	.013	.091	.129	.091	.116	.094
1960–1969	−.041	.042	.082	.044	.073	.089
1970–1979	−.038	.044	.084	.046	.113	.085
1980–1989	.014	.090	.128	.090	.144	.044*
1990–1999	.052	.124	.160	.124	.156	
2000–2009	.065	.136	.171	.138	.154	
2010–2019	.059	.132	.165	.135	.137	
2020–2029	.038	.112	.144	.117	.123	
2030–2039	.021	.097	.128	.103	.119	
2040–2049	.016	.092	.124	.099	.136	

* This average is over the period 1980–1988.

saving rates from now through 2030 and lower saving rates thereafter. For example, in Table 3 the 1987 base case predicted saving rates for the 2010s and 2040s are .065 and .026 respectively; the corresponding Table 6 values are .059 and .016.

IV. THE DEMOGRAPHIC TRANSITION AND FUTURE CURRENT ACCOUNTS

Given the openness of the U.S. economy, the significant saving rate changes predicted by the simulations presented in Tables 3–6 imply potentially large international capital flows and movements in the U.S. current account. The current account is a closely-watched measure in the area of international trade and competitiveness.

The current account surplus equals the difference between the accumulation of assets by Americans (including the government) and investment in the United States by Americans and foreigners. This difference, referred to as net foreign investment, indicates, if it is positive, that Americans are, on balance, saving enough to finance not only all investment in the United States, but also some investment abroad. If, on the other hand, net foreign investment is negative, saving by Americans is insufficient to finance all current investment in the United States and some current U.S. investment must be financed by foreigners. The implication of running current account deficits (having negative net foreign investment) is, therefore, that more of the capital at work in America will be owned by foreigners. Concern about foreigners buying up American capital has heightened in the 1980s as the nation ran quite substantial current account deficits when measured relative to net national product.

The demographic transition is likely to affect significantly future U.S. current account deficits both by altering U.S. saving and, therefore, the accumulation of assets by Americans and by altering the amount of investment in the United States. In the presence of significant international capital mobility, U.S. investment is determined, at the margin, not by the amount of U.S. saving, but rather by the international capital market. Given the rate of return that can be earned by investing abroad, investment will take place domestically up to the point that the return to capital in the United States equals the internationally determined rate of return. The domestic rate of return to investment will depend on the ratio of capital to labor. Hence, it is this capital-labor ratio that will adjust until the return to investment at home equals the return to investment elsewhere in the world. Given the supply of U.S. labor, which is determined in large part by demographics, investment (changes in capital) will occur up to the point that the U.S. capital-labor ratio is such as to yield the internationally determined rate of return. Thus demographics, by affecting the supply of labor, influences the amount of U.S. investment as well as U.S. saving. Since the current account deficit is the difference between U.S. investment and U.S. saving, demographics influences the current account as well.

Section II demonstrated that the demographic transition is likely, over time, to lower the rate of U.S. saving. Since the growth rate of U.S. labor supply will also decline, demographics will also lower the rate of U.S. investment (measured relative to *NNP*). The question is whether demographics will reduce saving by more than it reduces investment.

Table 7 presents the predicted values of the current account deficits for the next six decades divided by predicted net national product. The first three columns of the table provide estimates based on the assumption of constant world interest rates of 10, 7.5, and 5 percent, respectively. Each of these columns shows large predicted current account surpluses throughout the period, reversing the experience of current account deficits in the 1980s. The trend is toward improvement in the current account surpluses over the next 30 years and a gradual deterioration thereafter.

Such simulations may overstate the likely current account surpluses, because they ignore the demographic shifts that will be occurring simul-

TABLE 7
Predicted Current Account Surpluses Relative to Predicted Net National Product

| | World interest rate | | | | | |
| | Constant | | | Gradual decline | | |
Decade	.10	.075	.05	.10	.075	.05
1990–1999	.027	.025	.023	.025	.023	.021
2000–2009	.052	.050	.049	.050	.048	.047
2010–2019	.062	.062	.062	.061	.061	.060
2020–2029	.047	.047	.047	.045	.045	.045
2030–2039	.030	.029	.029	.028	.028	.027
2040–2049	.025	.025	.025	.024	.023	.023

taneously in other countries. Many of the mature Western economies will also experience population aging and associated increases in saving rates. Together, these increases in saving worldwide can be expected to depress world interest rates and reduce the outflow of funds from the United States. To consider this issue, we repeat the current account calculations just presented, this time assuming that the world interest rate falls gradually by 3 percentage points between 1990 and 2050 from the value initially assumed for the simulation. However, even such a significant drop in world interest rates only slightly diminishes the predicted surpluses over the period.

V. ALTERNATIVE EXPLANATIONS FOR THE RECENT DECLINE IN U.S. SAVING

While the demographic factors discussed in the previous sections may help predict the behavior of saving in the future, and may have contributed to the determination of saving in the past, they clearly cannot explain the behavior of saving in the 1980s. If our characterizations of the impact of demographics is correct, then there must have been other, major determinants of the rate of saving that pushed in the opposite direction during the 1980s, to offset the rise (relative to the '60s and '70s) in saving one would have predicted on the basis of demographic factors alone. This section of the paper briefly considers several alternative explanations that have been proposed for the decline in saving during the 1980s.

Government Consumption

One potential explanation for low U.S. saving in the 1980s that can be dismissed is that increased government consumption is to blame. Table 8 presents the ratio of government consumption to net national product based on both the corrected and uncorrected data. The corrected data indicate that the ratio of total government (federal, state, and local) consumption to NNP was only 0.5 percent higher (22.5 percent versus 22.0 percent) during the first half of the 1980s than it was during the period 1950 through 1979.

To measure the contribution of this small increase in the share of government spending out of NNP to the observed decline in the national saving rate, it is useful to consider the impact on national saving had the ratio of private consumption, C, to the fraction of output *not* absorbed by the government, NNP − G, remained the same. That is, we may define a saving rate out of private sector resources, which we shall, for convenience, call the *non-government* saving rate (NGSR),

$$NGSR = (NNP - G - C)/(NNP - G), \qquad (10)$$

and consider the impact of the increase in G/NNP holding this saving rate constant. This saving rate differs from the private saving rate defined above if the government's budget deficit, equal to government spending plus transfers less taxes, $G + R - T$, is not zero (see equation 7).

The non-government saving rate seems to be the appropriate measure of private saving to consider in thinking about changes in government consumption assuming 1) that government consumption is not a close substitute for private consumption and 2) that changes in government

TABLE 8
Net National and Non-Government Saving Rates, Corrected and Uncorrected

Period	Corrected measures			Uncorrected measures		
	National saving rate	Non-government saving rate	G/Y	National saving rate	Non-government saving rate	G/Y
1950–1959	.133	.167	.203	.092	.116	.211
1960–1969	.130	.166	.215	.089	.116	.226
1970–1979	.118	.152	.223	.085	.109	.222
1980–1985	.072	.093	.230	.050	.064	.223
1980–1988	na	na	na	.044	.057	.225

na: not available

consumption are not associated with changes in the intergenerational distribution of the burden of paying for government consumption.

Under these assumptions one would not expect a change in the fraction of output absorbed by government spending to affect the rate of private consumption out of national output left over after government consumption ($NNP - G$). If, instead, government consumption were a close substitute for private consumption, increases in government consumption would likely be offset by decreases in private consumption, leaving a smaller total impact on national consumption and saving. By making the first assumption, that the non-government saving rate is fixed, we are, therefore, biasing our analysis toward a larger impact of government consumption expenditure on national saving.

Changes in the intergenerational distribution of the burden of paying for government consumption that accompany changes in government consumption represent another reason that the nongovernment saving rate might change with changes in government consumption. We have discussed above the impact that such intergenerational changes might have on future saving, and will consider them again below. However, making the second assumption, and thereby ignoring the effects of such changes in the intergenerational distribution of the fiscal burden, seems most appropriate for discerning the effect of increased government consumption, per se, on total national saving.

It is easy to see that the small rise in the ratio of government saving to NNP could not, in itself, have had a very large impact on the national saving rate. Using the definitions of the national saving rate (NSR) given in expression (8) and the non-government saving rate ($NGSR$) given in expression (10), we have the relation

$$NSR = NGSR \times [1 - (G/NNP)]. \tag{11}$$

Expression (11) shows that a one percentage point increase in the ratio of G to NNP, holding the non-government saving rate constant, would reduce the national saving rate by only $NGSR$, or roughly 0.1 percent. Had the non-government saving rate remained constant in the 1980s at its average level for the period 1950–1979, the rise in government consumption to NNP in the 1980s would have reduced the uncorrected national saving rate for the 1980s from .089 (the average rate observed during the period 1950 through 1979) to .088. Hence, the non-government saving rate must also have declined substantially during the 1980s for national saving to have declined as it did. Table 8 presents corrected and uncorrected measures of the non-government saving rate, also repeating for convenience the national saving rates given in Table 2.

Regardless of whether one corrects the basic data for consumer durables and government investment, the non-government saving rate has fallen dramatically in the 1980s. According to the corrected data, it averaged 16.2 percent over the period 1950 through 1979, but only 9.3 percent from 1980 through 1985.

Deficits and Intergenerational Fiscal Policy

While the government did not consume much more of *NNP* in the 1980s than in the previous three decades, many content that the government, by running large deficits, shifted the burden of paying for government consumption from current to future generations. Such a generational policy, the argument goes, should induce a spending spree by current generations in response to their reduced tax bill. As an explanation for the observed decline in saving, however, this view encounters several problems.

The first problem concerns the measurement of the deficit itself. While there is no doubt that the official government deficit rose more rapidly in this decade than in any recent peacetime period, there is reason to doubt that the government's generational policy was, on balance, as redistributive to current generations as is commonly believed. A closer look at intergenerational policy shows that a good deal of what the federal government gave current generations with its right hand during the 1980s, it took away with its left. For example, the 1983 Social Security amendments reduced the future benefits of current young and middle age generations by an amount, in present value, roughly equal to their gain from the income tax cuts. If current young and middle age generations understand this change and expect it to be sustained in the future, they should view this loss in future income as requiring them to consume less now and save more for their old age.

Even if one doubts that most individuals make the kind of rational, present value calculations necessary to "see through" reported budget deficits to the underlying effects of current and expected future fiscal policies, there are other reasons to doubt that the deficit is to blame for our low rate of national saving.

The strongest case for deficits leading to reduced national saving can be made from a Keynesian perspective. The Keynesian argument goes like this: households base their consumption decisions on current disposable income; since the household saving rate is very close to zero, increases in disposable income associated with increases in government transfers or decreases in taxes will increase consumption nearly dollar for dollar, thereby reducing national saving considerably.

One problem with the Keynesian approach is that it does not provide a strong justification for the assumption that consumption is based primarily on current disposable income. One possible argument for such an assumption is that American households are liquidity constrained, which in everyday language means they have few liquid assets and consume everything they can get their hands on. Hence, if the government takes less from them in the form of taxes, they will consume today every dollar that would otherwise have gone to taxes. However, essentially every study of liquidity constraints has demonstrated that, at most, 20 percent of American households are liquidity constrained. Such liquidity-constrained households probably account for, at most, 10 percent of total U.S. consumption.

A second reason to doubt the importance of liquidity constraints is that the growth of consumption expenditures, at least in the last five years, has not been limited to non-durables and services, as one would expect if liquidity-constrained households were the cause of the increased consumption spending. (They would not choose to provide for future consumption by purchasing durables). The average over the last five years of the annual share of total expenditures accounted for by durables is slightly higher than it was in the period 1950 through 1979.

A third reason why the liquidity constraint argument doesn't square with the facts has to do with the composition of the reported deficit. Interest payments comprised much of the federal deficits in the 1980s. For example, in 1985, $130 billion of the $196 billion federal deficit represented interest payments. Since liquidity-constrained households obviously aren't bond holders, the key variable to consider for such households is how the difference between taxes and transfers (excluding interest payments) changed in the 1980s compared to the earlier period. And one should consider not simply how federal taxes less transfers have changed, but how this difference has changed for all governments combined. For all governments (federal, state, and local), the ratio of taxes plus transfers to *NNP* averaged .220 between 1980 and 1987. It averaged .226 for the 1970s, .239 for the 1960s, and .224 for the 1950s. Hence, the share of taxes less transfers to *NNP* was only slightly lower in this decade than in the previous three decades. In considering these figures it is also worth noting that the very slight decline in the 1980s in the ratio of net taxes to *NNP* primarily reflects a decline in corporate taxation (which should not affect liquidity-constrained households). In the 1980s corporate taxes represented only 8.1 percent of total government taxes. In comparison, they represented 15.2 percent of total taxes in the 1960s.

Finally, even if one ignores the problems with the liquidity constraint argument (that would suggest omitting the interest component of the deficit) and adopts the Keynesian assumption of a high marginal propensity to consume additions to disposable income caused by budget deficits, this still fails to explain the extent of the observed decline in the national saving rate. To see that this is so, it is useful to note that the national saving rate (*NSR*) as defined in (8) is related to the deficit, $D \, (= G + R - T)$ and the private saving rate (*PSR*) defined in expression (7) by the following identity:

$$NSR = PSR \times [1 - (G/NNP)] - (1 - PSR) \times (D/NNP). \quad (12)$$

Given the near constancy of the ratio of government consumption to *NNP* over the past several decades, one can conclude that, holding the private saving rate fixed, a one percentage point increase in the deficit-net national product ratio would decrease the national saving rate by $1 - PSR$, or about 0.9 percent. Given the increase of 2.7 percent in the deficit ratio during the 1980s over its average for the period 1950–1979, had the private saving rate remained constant at its 1950–1979 average of 10.9 percent, the national saving rate should have declined by about 2.4 percent during the 1980s. In fact, the national saving rate fell by much more, about 4.5 percent, from the period 1950–1979 to the 1980s.

This greater decline in saving is evident from the sharp declines in the personal and private saving rates during the 1980s, already shown in Table 2. Even if deficits relative to *NNP* had not increased in recent years, this pattern of private saving rates would have led to substantial declines in national saving.

To summarize, even under the most extreme Keynesian view of deficits, one that has a weak theoretical justification, one can attribute only part of the recent decline in national saving to government budget deficits. Under more realistic views of the Keynesian model or other, more plausible, theories of consumption, notably the Life-Cycle model, one would expect deficits to have much smaller effects on saving, since households would be predicted to consume only a small fraction of the increase in current disposable income provided by the tax cuts (Auerbach and Kotlikoff, 1987; Poterba and Summers, 1988).

Saving Disincentives

It is hard to argue that saving disincentives are responsible for the decline in saving in this decade since in the first half of this decade the federal government reduced many saving disincentives. Foremost among these was the steady reduction in marginal tax rates on household capital income, from a top rate of 70 percent in 1980 to 33 percent in 1988.

Some of the policies used to promote savings, such as the IRAs, were, unfortunately, poorly designed to produce new saving and quite possibly reduced rather than increased saving. Others, such as the move toward a consumption-oriented tax base associated with the adoption of the Accelerated Cost Recovery System were not in place for long enough to have had a significant effect on saving; simulation studies (e.g., Summers, 1981 and Auerbach and Kotlikoff, 1987) indicate that many government policies aimed at stimulating savings can have significant effects that are observed only after decades, rather than a few years.

Increases in the Stock Market

Most theories of consumption predict that households will increase their spending in response to an increase in wealth. Since the 1980s witnessed a significant increase in stock market wealth, this may have led to additional consumption. Because the increases in wealth are themselves excluded from national income account measures of income, this, in turn, would overstate the ratio of consumption to true income, and hence understate the true saving ratio.

However, the increases in consumption that may have occurred in response to the rising stock market can explain only a small part of the declining rate of national saving. By far the largest increase in real stock market wealth during the 1980s occurred in 1985, when household equity increased in value by $449 billion in excess of the inflation rate. For the period 1981–1986 as a whole, the cumulative increase in stock market wealth was roughly double this, about $900 billion. Assuming that households consume 3 percent of their wealth each year, a reasonable estimate based on past economic research, this would have accounted for an increase of consumption equal to $27 billion, or .6 percent of *NNP*, in 1986, with smaller increases in earlier years and (because of the crash in 1987) later years as well.

However, this estimate for the effect of wealth changes on U.S. saving is too high for the following reason. The stock market represents less than 15 percent of total U.S. wealth; for other assets there have, on net, been offsetting capital losses over the 1980s. If one adds together capital gains and losses for all U.S. assets net of liabilities over the period 1980 through 1988 the total capital gain is only $260 billion measured in 1988 dollars. This represents only 1.7 percent of total 1988 U.S. net wealth. In the absence of this cumulative capital gain the 1988 rate of private saving would have been 6.5 percent rather than 6.3 percent, a very modest difference indeed.

A Decline in Precautionary and Bequest Saving?

Another potential explanation for the decline in private saving may be the expansion of insurance which reduces the need for precautionary savings. The government today provides disability insurance, unemployment insurance, survivor insurance, earnings insurance (through the progressive tax structure), life span insurance (through its Social Security annuities), old age health insurance, nursing home insurance (through Medicaid) and poverty insurance (through its welfare programs). Economic research suggests that each of these forms of government insurance, while of great economic value, can have the undesired side effect of greatly reducing national savings. Untangling the savings effects of the provision of each of these forms of insurance is a formidable task, and one that is not likely to yield conclusive answers.

A related explanation for the decline in saving is a reduction in saving for bequests, which may tie in with the decline in the birth rate. At least half and possibly as much as two thirds of U.S. wealth can be traced not to life cycle saving for retirement, but rather to private bequests and other intergenerational transfers. It is hard to assess whether there has been a decline in the bequest motive for saving, but such a decline would not be surprising given the general deterioration of the family in the U.S. as evidenced by the dramatic postwar rise in the fraction of marriages ending in divorce and the dramatic postwar decline in the fraction of the elderly, even the infirm elderly, living with their children.

Much of the saving associated with bequests that occurred prior to 1970 may have reflected the absence of significant annuity insurance. In 1960 old age annuities were only a small component of retirement finances. Today, social security and private pension annuities are, more often than not, the major component of retirement finances. Annuitizing one's resources eliminates the possibility of leaving such resources to the next generation. In other words, many of the bequests that occurred in the past may have been unintended, and with annuity instruments now widely available, there is less scope for unintentional bequests. The counterpart of fewer unintentional bequests and the availability of annuity insurance is that one can consume more since annuities have eliminated the concern about spending one's resources too quickly; i.e., the availability of annuities may have reduced significantly precautionary savings in response to life span uncertainty.

Other Factors

There are several other factors that can be dismissed as possible explanations of the decline in U.S. saving in the 1980s. The business cycle is one such factor. While, as one would expect, each of the different saving rate measures was low during the recessionary period 1981–1983, the rate of saving did not recover during the subsequent and ongoing boom. For example, the national (uncorrected), private, and personal saving rates in 1987 were each lower than they were in 1982.

A second possible explanation is a reduction in income inequality in the 1980s. According to the Keynesian view, a reduction in income inequality would shift more income to the liquidity constrained poorer segment of society and induce greater national consumption. The problem with this line of argument is that income inequality increased rather than declined during the 1980s. According to the Congressional Budget Office (1987), the share of total U.S. disposable income received by the 5 percent of families with the highest disposable incomes was 18.9 percent in 1977, 20.1 percent in 1980, 23.2 percent in 1984, and 23.5 percent in 1988. The share of disposable income received by the poorest 30 percent of U.S. families was 8.6 percent in 1977, 8.5 percent in 1980, 7.6 percent in 1984, and 7.6 percent in 1988.

A third factor is the increase in female labor force participation that occurred during the 1980s. This factor should, however, have increased saving, since one would expect part of the increased earnings of females to be saved. The saving rate should also have increased since, at least in the life cycle model, the saving rate depends of the fraction of workers, who save, to retirees, who dissave. An offsetting possibility is that increased female labor force participation reduced the precautionary saving needed by single-earner couples in the event the single earner becomes unemployed.

VI. SUMMING UP

This paper suggests that demographic change may significantly alter our rate of national saving and our current account position over the next 50 years. The gradual aging of the population is predicted to lead to higher saving rates over the next three decades with declines in the rate of saving thereafter. Associated with these predicted saving rate changes is a predicted improvement in the U.S. current account position in the 1990s, with a very gradual deterioration during the subsequent decades.

While demographics is a potentially very important factor in explaining saving, it does not appear to explain the drop in the U.S. saving rate in the 1980s. Indeed, based on demographics alone, one would have predicted saving rates to be high and roughly equal in the 1950s and 1980s and considerably lower in the 1960s and 1970s. What happened to U.S. saving in the 1980s remains an intriguing puzzle.

APPENDIX

AI. Simulating the Effects of Demographics on Saving Rates

The method used to simulate the effects of demographic change on saving rates can be understood more precisely by looking at the following formula for the national saving rate in year t, S_t.

$$S_t = 1$$

$$- \frac{c_{40,m,b} \sum_{a=0}^{120} [R_{a,m}^c \theta_{a,m,t} + R_{a,f}^c \theta_{a,f,t}] + g_{y,b}\beta_{y,t} + g_{m,b}\beta_{m,t} + g_{o,b}\beta_{o,t} + \bar{g}_b}{k_{40,m,b} \sum_{a=0}^{120} [R_{a,m}^k \theta_{a,m,t} + R_{a,m}^k \theta_{a,f,t}] + e_{40,m,b} \sum_{a=0}^{120} [R_{a,m}^e \theta_{a,m,t} + R_{a,f}^e \theta_{a,f,t}]}$$

$$(A1)$$

The first term in the numerator of the ratio in (A1) is per capita private consumption in base year b. This is expressed as consumption per 40-year-old male in year b, $c_{40,m,b}$, multiplied by a summation. The terms $R_{a,m}^c$ and $R_{a,f}^c$ in the summation are, respectively, the ratios of average male and average female consumption at age a relative to the average consumption of a 40-year-old male. And the terms $\theta_{a,m,t}$ and $\theta_{a,f,t}$ are, respectively, the male and female shares of the population age a in year t. The two terms in the denominator of the ratio in (A1) are defined symmetrically, except that the first deals with capital income and the second deals with labor earnings. The terms $g_{y,b}$, $g_{m,b}$, $g_{o,b}$ and $\bar{g}_b$ are, respectively, the ratio of government consumption expenditure per young person (age 0 to 18), per middle age person (age 19 to 64), per old person (65 plus), and per capita. Finally, the terms $\beta_{y,t}$, $\beta_{m,t}$, and $\beta_{o,t}$ are, respectively, the fraction of the year t population that are young, middle age, and old.

Given base year values of $g_{y,b}$, $g_{m,b}$, $g_{o,b}$, $\bar{g}_b$, $c_{40,m,b}$, $e_{40,m,b}$, and $k_{40,m,b}$ and the values of the relative age-sex consumption, earnings, and capital income profiles (the $R_{a,m,t}^c$'s, $R_{a,f,t}^c$'s, $R_{a,m,t}^e$'s, $R_{a,f,t}^e$'s, $R_{a,m,t}^k$'s, and $R_{a,f,t}^k$'s) one can use equation (1) to determine how saving rates would change with changes in the age-sex composition of the population (the $\theta_{a,m,t}$'s, $\theta_{a,f,t}$'s, $\beta_{y,t}$'s, $B_{m,t}$'s, and $B_{o,t}$'s). The procedure for determining base year values of $c_{40,m,b}$, $e_{40,m,b}$, and $k_{40,m,b}$ is provided in equations (A2) through (A4).

$$C_b = c_{40,m,b} \sum_{a=0}^{120} [R_{a,m}^c P_{a,m,b} + R_{a,f}^c P_{a,f,b}] \qquad (A2)$$

$$E_b = e_{40,m,b} \sum_{a=0}^{120} [R_{a,m}^e P_{a,m,b} + R_{a,f}^e P_{a,f,b}] \qquad \text{(A3)}$$

$$YK_b = k_{40,m,b} \sum_{a=0}^{120} [R_{a,m}^k P_{a,m,b} + R_{a,f}^k P_{a,f,b}] \qquad \text{(A4)}$$

Equation (A2) indicates that total consumption in year b, C_b, can be expressed as the product of $c_{40,m,b}$ times the sum of the products of the age-sex consumption ratios and the levels of population in year b in a given age-sex category (the $P_{a,m,b}$'s). Equations (A3) and (A4) are the analogous expressions relating $e_{40,m,b}$ to total labor earnings, E_b and $k_{40m,b}$ to total base year capital income, YK_b. Given values of C_b, E_b, and YK_b as well as the terms within the summations of equations (A2), (A3), and (A4), these three equations can be solved for $c_{40,m,b}$, $e_{40,m,b}$, and $k_{40,m,b}$.

The procedure for finding $g_{y,b}$, $g_{m,b}$, $g_{o,b}$, and $\bar{g}_b$ is similar. Specifically, we used Auerbach et al.'s (1989) age-decomposition of government consumption expenditure to determine the values of $g_{y,b}$, $g_{m,b}$, $g_{o,b}$ and $\bar{g}_b$, which stand, respectively, for government consumption per person age 0–24, government consumption per person age 25–64, government consumption per person age 65+, and per capita non–age-specific government consumption, $\bar{g}_b$. Government consumption per capita in year t is then determined by multiplying these four values by their corresponding populations in year t and dividing by the total population in year t. Unfortunately, data are available only to calculate values of $g_{y,b}$, $g_{m,b}$, $g_{o,b}$, and $\bar{g}_b$ for the period of the mid-1980s. Hence, in the calculations presented below, these values are used regardless of the base year indicated.

For each base year the value of total private consumption (used in (A2) to solve for $c_{40,m,b}$) corresponds to the National Accounts figure (unadjusted for durables) for that year. In addition, base year net national product (again unadjusted) is divided between labor and capital income using the national accounts data on employee compensation and proprietorship income and assuming that the share of proprietorship income that represents payments for labor is the same as the ratio of aggregate labor income to net national product.

A2. Simulating the Effects of Demographics on the Current Account

To simulate the effects of demographics on the current account, we begin by assuming a value, r, of the world interest rate. Dividing 1987

capital income from the national income accounts by r gives us an estimate of 1987 U.S. assets, A_{1987}. To find A_{1988}, A_{1989}, through A_{2050} we use
the following formula:

$$A_{t+1} = A_t + s_t NNP_t \qquad (A5)$$

In (A5) A_t is assets at year t (e.g., 1987), s_t is the year t saving rate as
calculated in Section II above with 1987 as the base year, and NNP_t is net
national product in year t, which is also calculated as in Section II above
with 1987 as the base year; i.e., it is the sum of 1) average capital income
of a 40-year-old male in 1987 times the summations of the cross products
terms (the $R_{m,a}^k \theta_{m,a,t}$'s and the $R_{f,a}^k \theta_{f,a,t}$'s) plus 2) average labor income of a
40-year-old male in 1987 times the summations of the cross product
terms (the $R_{m,a}^e \theta_{m,a,t}$'s and the $R_{f,a}^e \theta_{f,a,t}$'s).

The level of the capital stock at time t is determined by assuming a
Cobb-Douglas net (of depreciation) production technology for U.S. domestic output, Y_t^d:

$$Y_t^d = DK_t^\alpha L_t^{1-\alpha} \qquad (A6)$$

where D is a coefficient whose value is determined in equation (A7), α is
capital's share of net national product, and L_t is the supply of labor in
year t. The value for α was determined from the National Accounts data.
The value of L_t is given by the second summation in the denominator of
equation (10). Since the marginal product of U.S. capital must equal the
world interest rate r, we have:

$$\alpha D \left[\frac{L_t}{K_t} \right]^{1-\alpha} = r \qquad (A7)$$

Given a value for r and K_{1987}, we insert the 1987 value of L_t and use (A7)
to solve for D. The value of K_{1987} is determined from the 1987 current
account reported in the national accounts. Specifically, $r(K_{1987} - A_{1987})$ is
set equal to the 1987 current account deficit less the 1987 trade account
(exports minus imports). This equation is then used to solve for K_{1987}.
Having determined the value of D in (A7), we use (A7) to predict values
of K_{1988} through K_{2050} by inserting the predicted values of L_t for the
appropriate year in question. Since the current account deficit in year t,
CA_t, is defined as:

$$CA_t = [K_t + 1 - A_t + 1] - [K_t - A_t] \qquad (A8)$$

we simply insert the predicted time paths of capital stocks and assets to determine the time path of CA_t.

REFERENCES

Abel, Andrew, Douglas Bernheim, and Laurence J. Kotlikoff. In progress, Fall 1989. "Do the Average and Marginal Propensities to Consume Rise with Age?"

Auerbach, Alan J. and Kevin Hassett. "Corporate Saving and Shareholder Consumption." In *The Economics of Saving*. D. Bernheim and J. Shoven, eds. University of Chicago Press, forthcoming.

Auerbach, Alan J. and Laurence J. Kotlikoff. 1987. *Dynamic Fiscal Policy*. Cambridge, England: Cambridge University Press.

Auerbach, Alan J., Laurence J. Kotlikoff, Robert P. Hagemann, and Giuseppe Nicoletti. 1989. "The Economic Dynamics of an Aging Population: The Case of Four OECD Countries." *OECD Staff Papers*.

Carroll, Chris and Lawrence H. Summers. 1989. "Consumption Growth Parallels Income Growth: Some New Evidence." Mimeo.

Congressional Budget Office. October 1987. *The Changing Distribution of Federal Taxes: 1975–1990*. Congress of the United States.

David, Paul and John Scadding. "Private Savings: Ultrarationality, Aggregation, and 'Denison's Law.' " *Journal of Political Economy*, March/April 1974, vol. 2, Part 1, pp. 225–49.

Kotlikoff, Laurence J. and Lawrence H. Summers. 1981. "The Role of Intergenerational Transfers in Aggregate Wealth Accumulation." *Journal of Political Economy*.

Poterba, James and Lawrence H. Summers. 1987. "Finite Lifetimes and the Effects of Budget Deficits on National Saving," *Journal of Monetary Economics*. Sept. pp. 369–91.

Summers, Lawrence H. 1981a. "Capital Taxation and Capital Accumulation in a Life Cycle Growth Model." *American Economic Review*. September 71:4:533–44.

IMPLICATIONS OF INTRODUCING U.S. WITHHOLDING TAXES ON FOREIGNERS' INTEREST INCOME

Lawrence H. Goulder
Stanford University and NBER

EXECUTIVE SUMMARY

This paper explores efficiency and equity issues related to the introduction of a withholding tax on foreigners' interest income from their investments in the U.S. Because of existing treaty obligations and tax-avoidance options, the effective tax rate of any practicable withholding tax is likely to be considerably below its statutory rate. A statutory 30 percent U.S. withholding tax on portfolio interest, if not accompanied by similar (retaliatory) tax measures introduced by foreign governments, appears to yield aggregate domestic welfare gains. The gains are attributable to U.S. financial market power stemming from the large share represented by the U.S. of world financial transactions and from the imperfect substitutability between U.S. and foreign securities in port-

This paper was prepared for the NBER Conference on Tax Policy and the Economy, Washington, D.C., November 14, 1989. I am grateful to Lans Bovenberg, Don Brean, Daniel Frisch, Alberto Giovannini, Harry Grubert, Jim Hines, Charles McLure, Jack Mutti, and Larry Summers for helpful suggestions. I also thank Margaret Lewis of the Foreign Returns Analysis Section of the Internal Revenue Service for providing income and tax data, and Philippe Thalmann for both useful comments and excellent research assistance.

folios. Gains also derive from effects on domestic saving. The withholding tax leads to only a temporary improvement in the U.S. trade balance and in aggregate exports. The ultimate deterioration of the trade balance is closely related to effects of the tax on international interest flows.

If foreign governments respond in kind to a U.S. withholding tax initiative, the combined effect is a decline in U.S. residents' aggregate welfare. Foreign retaliation enlarges the global efficiency losses associated with a new U.S. withholding tax.

The equity arguments for the withholding tax are mixed. Restricting the application of the tax to investors from countries that already impose similar measures may have more justification on fairness grounds than applying the tax to all foreign investors. An attraction of the tax is its ability to discourage capital flight to the U.S. and related tax evasion; however, other policies with less serious efficiency costs might be equally effective in addressing tax evasion problems.

I. INTRODUCTION

In the past two decades, the U.S. economy has become significantly more open to international flows of financial capital. As a percent of GNP, gross imports of financial capital—from foreigners' direct and portfolio investments in the U.S.—rose from 0.5 percent in 1965 to 5.0 percent in 1985. These inflows have gradually but significantly altered the pattern of capital ownership in the U.S.: while less than 3 percent of U.S.-located capital was foreign-owned 20 years ago, today foreigners own approximately 7.5 percent of the domestic capital stock.

These developments have given new impetus to discussions about the appropriate tax treatment of foreign-owned capital. Much of the interest income generated in this country now accrues to foreigners, adding importance to the question as to whether such income should be subject to U.S. taxation. Foreign income from U.S. sources has long been subject to a U.S. statutory 30 percent "withholding" tax. However, in July 1984, a major component of the tax was removed with the elimination of withholding taxes on foreigners' interest income from U.S. sources. Recent events have intensified the debate over whether the U.S. should again include foreigners' interest income in the U.S. tax base.

Advocates of taxing foreigners' interest income emphasize that this policy would help diminish the "twin deficits" problem now faced by the U.S. The revenue raised by expanding the withholding tax would help reduce the government budget deficit; at the same time, by discouraging capital inflows, taxing foreigners' interest income would reduce the capital account imbalance and thereby help reduce the trade deficit. Discouraging capital inflows, it is argued, reduces demands for dollar-denominated assets, helping to lower the exchange rate value of the dollar and enhancing the international competitiveness of export-oriented domestic industries.

Proponents also maintain that an expanded withholding tax would alleviate problems of tax evasion and capital flight that are particularly troubling for less developed countries. Many foreign individuals and firms now invest in the U.S. in order to escape taxation at home; although in many cases the income from such investments is officially subject to taxation by the home country, such investments are difficult to monitor and evasion is relatively easy. By reducing incentives to invest in the U.S., it is argued, an expanded withholding tax would discourage capital flight from many emerging nations and reduce tax evasion.

Opponents of the policy initiative assert that a tax on foreigners' interest income would in fact raise very little revenue. They point out that bilateral treaties would oblige the U.S. to exempt capital income earned by investors from several nations; they also indicate that even in cases where the U.S. could apply the tax, there are many ways that investors could rechannel their investments to escape taxation. Critics also argue that the tax would curtail domestic capital formation. To attract foreign investors, before-tax interest rates would have to rise (to offset the tax), raising the cost of capital to domestic firms and reducing incentives to invest in plant and equipment.

Many also worry that expanding the withholding tax would give rise to retaliation by other governments, perhaps by way of similar withholding measures, and higher tax burdens on U.S. residents. Others point out that the imposition of withholding taxes—whether by the U.S. or other nations—constitutes an unfortunate departure from the residence principle of taxation according to which governments tax only their own residents. Expanding the withholding tax represents a further departure from this principle. These critics assert that abiding by the residence principle is worthwhile because doing so not only avoids double taxation but also tends to promote a more efficient international allocation of resources.

This paper investigates these issues. The next section begins the investigation by providing some historical background; here the focus is on the previous experience with withholding taxes in the U.S., although some atttention is paid to West Germany's recent experience with such taxes. Section III then provides a framework for evaluating the effects of an expanded U.S. withholding tax. This framework guides the design and interpretation of simulation experiments, reported in Section IV, which allow for quantitative assessments of positive and normative effects of such a policy. The fifth section enlarges upon the previous analysis by considering issues of international fairness and possibilities for international policy coordination. The final section offers conclusions.

II. PREVIOUS EXPERIENCE WITH WITHHOLDING TAXES

A. Statutory and Effective Rates in the U.S.[1]

Prior to July 1984, the U.S. levied a 30 percent withholding tax on U.S.-sourced income paid to non-resident aliens or foreign corporations. The tax applied to several forms of portfolio income, including interest and dividend income.[2] However, for several reasons the effective rate was less than the statutory rate. First, several types of interest income were exempt. Interest paid on deposits with domestic banks (including certificates of deposit), savings and loan associations, and similar financial institutions was exempt. The law also exempted interest paid by U.S. corporations earning less than 20 percent of gross income from sources within the U.S., interest paid by insurance companies, and the original issue discount on instruments with a maturity of less than six months (for example, short-term commercial paper and U.S. Treasury bills).

A number of tax treaties further reduced the effective rate. Treaties with 16 countries, including West Germamy and the United Kingdom, assured that residents of these countries paid no U.S. withholding taxes. Residents of 12 other nations faced withholding rates below the statutory rate as a result of bilateral arrangements between their governments and the U.S. government. Other treaty arrangements allowed rate reductions for certain types of income that otherwise would have been subject to the tax.[3]

The revenue potential of the tax was further weakened as a consequence of Internal Revenue Service rulings that enabled U.S. corporate lenders to avoid the withholding tax by setting up finance subsidiaries in

---

[1] This subsection draws significantly from Papke (1989), which examines the previous U.S. experience in detail.

[2] The tax does not apply to income directly connected with the taxpayer's conduct of trade or business within the U.S. Such income is taxed separately and is treated as if it were received by a U.S. citizen or corporation.

[3] See Lewis (1986) for a detailed discussion of treaty arrangements, U.S.-sourced income received, and withholding taxes paid by country.

the Netherlands Antilles.[4] The tax was typically avoided by the subsidiary's issuing a Eurobond, free of tax, to a foreign investor, and then funneling the bond revenues to the U.S. parent corporation. IRS rulings in 1974 effectively authorized this practice, even though in these circumstances the subsidiary acted merely as a conduit for the parent. This channel enabled investors from countries without favorable treaty arrangements to purchase U.S. debt without facing the withholding tax.[5]

By 1983, Eurobond issues through the Netherlands Antilles represented nearly all new U.S. corporate bond issues abroad. In that year, interest payments to recipients in the Netherlands Antilles (on previously issued bonds) represented over 33 percent of total interest payments to foreigners. The importance of this tax-avoidance channel gives credence to the comment that the U.S. treaty with the Netherlands Antilles was a "one-way treaty with the world."

Thus, exemptions for certain types of securities, numerous treaty arrangements, and one large loophole greatly eroded the base of U.S. withholding tax. Table 1 shows income payments to foreigners and taxes withheld during the period 1981–1986. Prior to July 1984, the statutory rate on both interest and divided income was 30 percent. However, the table indicates that from 1981 to 1983, the average tax rate on all U.S.-sourced portfolio income ranges from 6.3 to 7.6 percent, far below the statutory 30 percent rate. The rate on dividends (11.6–12.4 percent) was higher than the rate on interest income (2.1–3.0 percent) during the three-year period. The differences reflect the Netherlands Antilles tax-avoidance option (which applied to interest) and the tendency of treaties to specify larger rate reductions for interest payments.

In July 1984, the U.S. repealed the withholding tax on foreigners' portfolio interest as part of the Deficit Reduction Act. The figures for 1985 in Table 1 indicate that the repeal had relatively little influence on the effective tax rate on foreigners' interest income: most of this income already could escape the tax before repeal. On the other hand, repeal had two very significant effects on the method of issuing debt to foreigners. First, it led to a surge in *direct* sales of debt to non-residents. Quarterly sales of U.S. bonds abroad never exceeded 0.3 billion from the

---

[4] The Netherlands Antilles is a Caribbean nation comprising the six islands Aruba, Bonnaire, Curacao, St. Maarten, St. Eustatius, and Saba.

[5] Many investors from countries whose treaties with the U.S. would have enabled them to avoid withholding still preferred the Eurobond market. This was the case because Eurobonds could be purchased anonymously; in contrast, to escape withholding by directly purchasing a U.S. bond and taking advantage of favorable treaty terms required that the investor provide information about his or her address and country of residence at every interest payment.

TABLE 1
Income Payments and Tax Withheld, 1981–1986

	All portfolio income			Dividends			Interest			Other		
	Income	Tax withheld	Avg. tax rate	Income	Tax withheld	Avg. tax rate	Income	Tax withheld	Avg. tax rate	Income	Tax withheld	Avg. tax rate
1981	9.56	.73	.076	4.27	.50	.116	3.36	.10	.028	1.93	.14	.070
1982	10.62	.76	.071	4.55	.54	.118	5.13	.15	.030	0.94	.07	.074
1983	11.06	.70	.063	4.17	.52	.124	5.91	.13	.021	0.98	.06	.057
1984	17.11	.97	.057	5.62	.66	.118	10.04	.21	.021	1.45	.10	.140
1985	17.50	.94	.054	5.05	.57	.112	9.85	.19	.020	2.60	.18	.069
1986	21.81	1.15	.053	6.51	.71	.110	11.78	.23	.020	3.53	.21	.059

Notes: Sources of data are Department of Treasury, Internal Revenue Service, *Compendium of Studies of International Income and Taxes, 1979–1983;* and *SOI Bulletin,* Fall 1985, 1986, 1987, and 1988.

Income and tax withheld are in billions of current dollars. Income is gross of taxes withheld. "Other" income consists mainly of rents, royalties, and personal service income. Taxes withheld do not include withholding by foreign governments or foreign government agents.

first quarter of 1982 to the second quarter of 1984; in contrast, such sales totaled $8.4 billion in the first quarter following repeal of the tax on portfolio interest and have averaged more than $6 billion since then. The second main effect was the complete elimination of the use of Netherlands Antilles finance subsidiaries to issue U.S. corporate debt.[6] This complex tax-avoidance procedure was no longer necessary.

B. The Recent West German Experience

The U.S. experience reveals the substantial responsiveness of borrowers to changes in international tax rules. Recent events in West Germany also indicate a high degree of responsiveness to tax changes, in this case displayed primarily by the lender side of the market. In the fall of 1987, the West German government announced that a withholding tax on interest income would go into effect in January 1989. The tax would apply to both resident and non-resident investors in German bond markets. While German domestic bonds (including government bonds) were subject to the tax, foreign securities, including foreign Deutschemark bonds, were exempt. Both resident (West German) and non-resident investors tended to shun the German market soon after the announcement of the tax. In contrast, Deutschemark bonds issued by foreign borrowers were much in demand. The February 1989 *Report of the Deutsche Bundesbank* stated that the key factor behind the shift toward the foreign bond market by domestic investors "was the fact that these bonds are not subject to withholding tax on interest income." Foreign investors also tended to shift toward the foreign bond market.[7]

These shifts in demand were accompanied by changes in the interest rate differentials between German bonds and other similar securities. While the yield on German Federal bonds typically had been 0.25 to 0.5 percent below the yield on foreign Deutschemark bonds, rates on the former securities rose above those on the foreign bonds beginning in January 1988 (soon after the announcement of the withholding tax).

In April 1989, the German government announced that the withholding tax would be repealed beginning July 1, 1989.[8] The news was fol-

---

[6] For details on these effects, see Papke (1989).

[7] Demand for most types of German bonds sagged, with the exception of German domestic bank bonds, most of which were purchased by German savings banks. Interest received by savings banks were exempt from the withholding tax. For details, see *Monthly Report of the Deutsche Bundesbank* 41 (2), February 1989.

[8] In repealing the tax, the government adopted the position taken by the Deutsche Bundesbank and various industry groups that withholding had had serious adverse effects on monetary policy and the capital market and therefore could no longer be defended. See *Report of the Deutsche Bundesbank for the Year 1988*.

lowed by significant responses in both demands and interest rate differentials. Both domestic and foreign investors appeared to shift their portfolios toward the German domestic bond market. For example, while foreign investors reduced their holdings of German public bonds by 7.5 billion marks in the first three months of 1989, in April they took up public bonds totaling more than 4 billion marks. The Deutsche Bundesbank attributed this change to the announced abolition of the withholding tax.[9] The changes were accompanied by changes in interest differentials. In May 1989, the yield on German Federal bonds fell below that on foreign Deutschemark bonds for the first time since December 1987.

C. Lessons and Revenue Implications

The U.S. and West German experiences yield a number of insights regarding the potential effects of prospective changes in the U.S. withholding tax. The U.S. experience brings out the degree to which borrowers may alter financial practices in order to provide untaxed financial instruments and thereby avoid the need to offer higher yields to investors. In West Germany, tax avoidance was accomplished less by firms' changing their methods of financing and more by lenders' shifting away from the securities offered by German firms or banks.

Together, these experiences reveal a substantial potential for tax-avoidance behavior on both sides of the market. The attractiveness of expanding the withholding tax depends importantly on its revenue yield, and if a U.S. tax on foreign interest is going to yield significant revenues, the tax will have to be more difficult to escape than its predecessor.

Could a U.S. withholding tax on foreigners' interest be implemented in a way that yields significant revenues? Certainly in one important respect, the revenue potential of the tax could be enhanced easily—by proscribing the establishment of finance subsidiaries (in the Netherlands Antilles or elsewhere) for the purpose of avoiding withholding. This would not pose administrative problems, and would substantially shrink, if not eliminate, an important loophole.[10]

However, broadening the base of the tax might prove to be more difficult. Extensive base broadening would require renegotiating exist-

---

[9] See *Monthly Report of the Deutsche Bundesbank* 41 (7), July 1989.

[10] It is unlikely that the prohibition could be made air-tight, given the difficulty of establishing whether the parent company's main reason for creating a given subsidiary was tax avoidance.

ing treaties that exempt residents of certain countries from U.S. withholding. In view of the political costs of such initiatives, this may not be a realistic option. The success of this option would also be dampened to the extent that some foreigners reduced their tax obligations by setting up "tax residences" in countries other than their main country of residence—namely, in countries with particularly advantageous treaties with the U.S. This suggests that the revenue potential of a withholding tax on foreigners' portfolio interest will be compromised so long as there are a few countries whose treaties with the U.S. continue to offer their residents particularly favorable withholding rates.

Another potential way to expand the revenue of the tax is to broaden the domain of financial instruments covered by the tax. A main candidate for such broadening is interest on bank deposits. However, attempts to broaden the tax in this way might encounter substantial opposition. Some have questioned the advisability of extending the tax to interest received on bank deposits in view of the fact that some depositors are financial intermediaries, both lenders and borrowers. The claim is that banks and other firms engaged in financial intermediation should be given a tax deduction on interest paid to offset the tax on interest received. It is argued that for such firms, a tax on gross interest amounts to a tax on gross income and is effectively a tax on financial intermediation itself. This is considered unfair to the intermediaries; only a tax on net income is considered legitimate.[11] However, it might be difficult for the U.S. to administer a tax that applies only to net interest. Many financial intermediaries would claim interest deductions for payments made to foreign investors, and such payments would be difficult for the U.S. government to verify.

These considerations motivate some calculations of the potential additional revenues from expanding the withholding tax. First, suppose withholding were expanded by introducing a tax on portfolio interest with the same features (similar tax base, similar loopholes) as the portfolio interest tax that applied prior to July 1984. Table 1 showed that the effective rate on portfolio interest changed very little after repeal. In 1983, the effective rate was 2.1 percent; in 1985 and 1986, 2.0 percent. A reasonable assumption is that resurrecting the type of interest withholding that applied prior to repeal would raise the effective rate by 0.1 percentage points; such an increase in the effective rate implies an additional $.02 billion for the year 1990, assuming gross portfolio interest

---

[11] It may be noted that the West German withholding tax exempted "domestic bank bonds," most of which were purchased by German savings banks.

payments to foreigners in 1990 of $20.9 billion.[12] Alternatively, one might project the revenue effects by assuming that the extension of withholding restores the average rate on *all* U.S. source portfolio income to the rate which applied prior to repeal. This alternative approach suggests that extending the withholding tax would imply an additional $.2 billion for the year 1990.[13] These simple calculations suggest that an interest withholding tax of the type that applied prior to July 1984 would not yield significant revenues. Moreover, these calculations probably overstate the *net* revenue effect from such an expansion of the tax: to the extent that the tax on interest income induces a rise in before-tax U.S. interest rates, it raises the value of interest deductions from the U.S. corporate income tax, implying an offsetting revenue loss.[14]

Some simple further calculations give a rough idea of the potential additional revenues that might be generated by removing loopholes and broadening the base of the portfolio interest tax. These calculations will be crude in that they will assume the tax does not alter the level and composition of gross income payments to foreigners.[15] The implications of removing the Netherlands Antilles loophole can be gauged by raising the effective rate to Netherlands Antilles recipients from 0.44 percent—the effective rate on income to recipients in this country in 1983—to 7.69 percent—the average effective rate to recipients from other countries.[16] Doing so implies additional revenues of $0.49 billion. The effects of removing the favorable provisions of treaties can be assessed in similar fashion: by replacing the 1983 average effective rate to treaty countries (7.50 percent) with the average rate that applied to non-treaty countries

[12] The value of 1990 interest payments to foreigners was projected from the actual payments level in 1987 assuming an annual growth rate of 22.5 percent, the average annual rate over the period 1981–1987.

[13] This alternative approach assumes that the composition of foreigners' holdings of U.S. assets would be the same after reintroducing interest withholding as it was in 1983 (prior to repeal). In 1983, the average effective withholding tax rate (Table 1) was 6.3 percent; in 1987, the most recent year for which such data are available, the average effective rate was 5.7 percent. If restoring interest withholding raised the overall rate by 0.6 percentage points in 1990, it would thereby generate $0.2 billion, assuming gross income payments to foreigners in 1990 of $35.1 billion. The 1990 gross income figure was projected from the actual payments level in 1987 assuming an annual growth rate of 15.5 percent, the average annual rate over the period 1981–1987.

[14] See Brean (1984) for an examination of this issue.

[15] These calculations probably overstate potential additional revenues, since agents are likely to alter savings instruments and shift methods of financing in order to reduce their tax obligations.

[16] Figures for average withholding tax rates for different countries were obtained from Carson (1985). Withholding by foreign governments or foreign withholding agents is not considered.

(10.01 percent). This implies additional revenues of $0.96 billion.[17] Finally, withholding interest payments on bank deposits could bring in further revenues. Applying an effective rate of 30 percent to estimated U.S. bank deposit interest to non-bank foreigners in 1990 implies an additional $3.1 billion in revenues.[18]

Thus, these crude calculations suggest that expanding the withholding tax might raise from $0.02 to $4.75 billion in additional annual revenues, depending on the extent of loophole-closing and base-broadening. Bank deposits appear to represent the largest potential source of new revenues.

Of course, the revenue potential of an expanded withholding tax is only one of several important considerations relevant to assessing the effects of the policy option on economic well-being. The next section brings out other critical considerations.

III. A FRAMEWORK FOR EVALUATING WITHHOLDING TAXES

This section presents a framework for analyzing potential effects of changes in withholding taxes on the domestic economy. The focus is on domestic welfare.

We begin with the case that is simplest to analyze: here we abstract from the possibility of U.S. market power in world capital markets and from pre-existing taxes on domestic saving or domestic investment. We also abstract from the presence of tax credits offered by foreign governments and from the possibility of retaliation (for example, imposing new taxes on U.S. residents' investments abroad) by foreign governments. Subsection B below extends the analysis to consider these complications.

A. *The Simplest Case*

In the simple case considered here, the U.S. is regarded as a price taker in international markets for financial capital. In Figure 1, the horizontal line S_{F1} represents the original supply curve of financial capital; in keeping with the price-taker assumption, the supply is perfectly elastic at the

---

[17] To avoid double-counting, the additional income is calculated by employing an adjusted average rate for treaty countries. This rate is calculated after adjusting taxes paid by Netherlands Antilles recipients to incorporate the assumption that the finance subsidiary loophole had been removed.

[18] Gross interest payments on bank deposits were projected from data on demand and time deposits of non-bank foreigners published in the 1985 *Treasury Bulletin.* An interest rate of 8 percent was assumed.

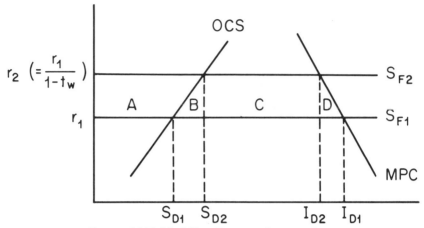

FIGURE 1. *Effects of Withholding Taxes: The Simplest Case*

world interest rate r_1. The downward and upward sloping lines represent the marginal product of capital (MPC) and opportunity cost of saving (OCS) as functions of the levels of domestic investment and domestic saving, respectively.[19] In the absence of a withholding tax and of other taxes, equilibrium in the capital market is established with domestic saving equal to S_{D1}, domestic investment equal to I_{D1}, and imports of capital equal to $I_{D1} - S_{D1}$.

If the U.S. alters this environment by imposing a withholding tax, the pre-tax return offered to foreign investors must rise to $r_2 = r_1/(1 - t_w)$, where t_w is the withholding tax rate; the increase in the pre-tax return is necessary to make the after-tax return to foreign investors comparable to the return these investors could obtain elsewhere. Thus, the foreign supply curve rises to S_{F2}. The higher gross rate reduces investment demands to I_{D2} and stimulates a higher level of domestic saving, S_{D2}.[20] Hence imports of financial capital fall.

[19] It is not necessary to specify the time frame for the saving and investment schedules employed here. What is critical is that OCS and MPC respectively take into account all future consumption alternatives and the productiveness of a current investment over all future points in time.

[20] We assume here that U.S. firms are unable to discriminate between domestic and foreign lenders when they issue securities. Thus, the higher gross return must be offered to both classes of lenders. This assumption seems well substantiated by empirical observation.

This partial equilibrium analysis assumes that increases in the after-tax interest rate bring about a higher volume of saving. In general equilibrium, this need not be the case

The tax has the following welfare effects. The higher returns offered to domestic savers yield a welfare gain to these savers which is represented by the area A. Domestic firms face higher costs of borrowing, and suffer a welfare loss represented by regions A, B, C, and D taken together. The revenues collected by the tax yield a gain to taxpayers which is represented by C.[21] In the aggregate, the tax yields a domestic welfare loss of $B + D$. B is the dead-weight loss associated with the domestic economy's having to finance $S_{D2} - S_{D1}$ of domestic investments at a rate higher than the world interest rate, r_1, and yet not collecting any withholding tax on these investments. D is the dead-weight loss associated with no longer undertaking marginal investments $I_{D1} - I_{D2}$, whose returns exceed the world interest rate.

This initial, simple analysis indicates that if the U.S. is a price taker in international capital markets and if one abstracts from possible complications posed by foreign tax credits and other taxes, then imposing a withholding tax will not improve aggregate domestic welfare. The analysis here is similar to that which applies to the introduction of an import tariff in an economy that is a price taker in commodity markets. Of course, the withholding tax redistributes wealth and welfare, and this enables some agents—for example, savers and taxpayers—to gain. And certain U.S. industries may benefit (in terms of profitability or sales) from the tax change. Export-oriented industries, in particular, may gain. The reduction in capital imports occasioned by the tax reduces demands for dollar-denominated assets and thus tends to make the dollar cheaper in international exchange markets. This will tend to benefit domestic industries oriented toward the export market, at least initially.[22]

(see, for example, Bovenberg (1989a)). Possibilities of shifts in the saving schedule as a result of general equilibrium effects do not alter the aggregate welfare analysis presented here.

[21] The taxpayer's gain may occur in one of two ways. The tax revenues may permit the government to maintain the same real expenditure while lowering other taxes by the amount raised by the withholding tax. Alternatively, the government may use the revenues to provide additional goods and services valued by taxpayers. In this latter case, C accurately represents the welfare gain to taxpayers only if the value to them of a dollar of additional public expenditure equals the value to them of a dollar of private expenditure. If the government is inefficient in its use of tax revenues, the gains to taxpayers will be lower, but the essential aggregate welfare conclusions from the analysis do not change.

[22] Because the withholding tax reduces domestic investment, the policy ultimately implies a lower capital stock than otherwise would be the case. Over the longer term, the lower stock may imply reduced real incomes and reduced demands for the products of all industries, including export-oriented industries. Using a dynamic simulation model, Goulder and Eichengreen (1989a) and Bovenberg and Goulder (1989) find that, because of capital accumulation effects, investment-oriented policies have opposite implications for the output and profitability of export industries in the short and long run.

B. Complications

1. U.S. Market Power.   The above analysis assumed that the U.S. is a small actor in world financial markets. This clearly is not the case. In 1988, securities issued by the U.S. amounted to $47.2 billion, approximately 14.3 percent of the total value of securities issued by the OECD nations.[23] This large share of the supply side of the market suggests considerable monopsony power: changes in U.S. demands for investible funds (supplies of securities) are likely to have a significant effect on world interest rates.

The large market share is not the only potential source of market power. Such power also arises if foreign investors cannot perfectly substitute securities issued by the U.S. for foreign securities. Under these circumstances, foreign interest rates and the U.S. rate (after withholding) will not be brought to equality following the introduction of a withholding tax: investors will not sufficiently shift toward foreign securities to drive the foreign rate down to match the U.S. rate net of withholding. Hence imperfect substitutability also grants market power to the U.S. because it allows the withholding tax to drive down U.S. interest rates (after withholding). In the extreme case where foreign investors cannot substitute foreign securities for U.S. securities to any degree, the withholding tax need not cause pre-tax rates to rise at all: that is, the after-tax rate can fall by the full amount of the tax without causing any reduction in the supply of foreign funds to the U.S.[24]

For a nation with the power to influence after-tax interest rates, it is no longer the case that a withholding tax will necessarily reduce aggregate welfare. As shown in the appendix, the aggregate welfare effects now must take account of the effects of withholding on the domestic after-tax rate and the foreign interest rate. The larger is a nation's share of the world capital market, the greater its ability to drive down interest rates. If the nation is a net capital importer, reduced interest rates tend to reduce the costs of net capital imports. This implies a welfare benefit that to some degree will offset the adverse aggregate welfare effects of introducing withholding. In contrast, for a net capital exporting country, larger market share tends to reduce the attractiveness of withholding by reducing the returns from net capital exports.

Imperfect substitutability generally makes withholding more attrac-

---

[23] This information was obtained from *OECD Financial Statistics, Part 1, Financial Statistics Monthly,* January 1989.

[24] This abstracts from income effects. By reducing foreigners' incomes, the withholding tax could depress the overall level of foreign saving and thereby exert some compensating upward influence on world interest rates.

tive. This is the case because it generally allows the domestic after-tax interest rate—the rate paid to import capital—to fall by more than the world interest rate—the rate received on exported capital. Thus, the lower the substitutability between domestic and foreign securities, the higher the *net* interest income following the introduction of withholding.[25]

2. Foreign Tax Credits.   The tax systems of many nations include provisions which would permit their residents to credit withholding taxes paid to the U.S. against tax obligations to the foreign government. Indeed, all of the OECD nations offer some type of credit for taxes paid by their residents to other governments, although in many cases the credit provisions are rather restrictive.

The presence of foreign tax credits can substantially alter the effects of U.S. withholding taxes. If marginal foreign investors in the U.S. are eligible for full crediting of the withholding tax, then imposing the tax in the U.S. will lead to no change in the pretax rate of return offered on U.S. securities. The tax payment to the U.S. government in this case is fully offset by a lowered tax liability to the relevant foreign government. The overall return to the foreign investor (net of U.S. and foreign taxes) is unchanged.

Under these circumstances, the withholding tax would have no first-order effect on domestic pre-tax interest rates or on the level of domestic saving and investment. What the tax accomplishes is a transfer of revenues from foreign nations to the U.S. If one believes that foreign governments would not respond to this U.S. initiative by imposing similar withholding taxes on U.S. investors, then the U.S. withholding tax appears quite attractive from the point of view of domestic welfare.

However, it is important to note that these results obtain only if the marginal foreign investor is eligible for the tax credit. Even if a large number of investors in U.S. securities can take advantage of the credit, if the marginal investor cannot, then domestic borrowers will need to increase pre-tax interest rates to attract the necessary additional lenders. In this case, introducing U.S. withholding directly affects the equilibrium in the domestic loanable funds markets, as in the cases previously described.

3. Pre-existing Taxes on Domestic Saving or Domestic Investment.   The previous analysis abstracted from important prior taxes on domestic

---

[25] As indicated in the appendix, evaluating the welfare implications of lower asset substitutability also requires consideration of the effects of lower substitutability on the levels of capital imports and exports.

saving and investment. The U.S. individual income tax drives a wedge between the gross and net return to saving by domestic households. The U.S. corporation income tax (including depreciation provisions) imposes a wedge between the gross and net return (at the level of the firm) from investments.[26]

In the presence of these other taxes, introducing a withholding tax may have quite different welfare implications from those originally derived. Prior taxes influence both the aggregate welfare impact and the distribution of the gains and losses. As shown in the appendix, the implications of prior saving taxes are different from those of prior taxes on investment. Prior taxes on (subsidies to) saving exert a positive (negative) influence on the net welfare impact of a withholding tax. To the extent that a withholding tax raises interest rates to domestic savers, it may stimulate additional domestic saving. This enables the saving tax to bring in more revenue. The additional revenue from the saving tax corresponds to a welfare gain. The welfare benefit occurs because taxes on saving cause the marginal social opportunity cost of a given level of saving to fall below the marginal social benefits (private return plus value of taxes) associated with that level of saving: at the margin, a unit of saving is worth more to individuals and taxpayers than its cost in terms of foregone consumption. Hence, there are welfare gains that stem from the increase in domestic saving induced by the withholding tax.

Similar considerations indicate that prior taxes on (subsidies to) investment reduce (increase) the appeal of withholding. Higher interest rates from the imposition of withholding tend to discourage domestic investment. In the presence of investment taxes, the decline in investment implies an additional welfare loss because, with such taxes, the marginal social benefit from investment exceeds its marginal social cost. Saving and investment taxes alter the distributional implications of a withholding tax by changing the relative magnitudes of domestic saving and investment in the initial equilibrium prior to the introduction of withholding.

4. Substitutions between Taxed and Untaxed U.S. Securities. As indicated in Section II, it is unlikely that any practicable U.S. withholding tax would effectively cover all U.S. securities. Assets might escape the tax

---

[26] For a detailed discussion of these "wedges," see King and Fullerton (1984). Sinn (1988) analyzes these issues in an open-economy context. Accelerated depreciation and other favorable tax provisions applied to investment raise the possibility that the overall wedge posed by investment-side tax policies may be negative (see Sinn [1988]).

by substitution activities undertaken by either borrowers or lenders. The use of Netherlands Antilles finance subsidiaries represented borrowers' substituting one financing channel for another in order to avoid the tax. Foreign investors' substituting untaxed U.S. certificates of deposit for taxed corporate bonds exemplifies a tax-avoidance response on the lender side of the market. Either type of substitution implies lower effective withholding tax rate than that employed in the previous analysis. In the polar case of perfect substitutability, the effective rate is zero: the introduction of the tax precipitates a complete switching to untaxed securities, so there is no first-order change in the equilibrium levels of domestic saving or investment.

How much substitution is possible? This depends both on the design of the tax and on preferences. Tax legislation might proscribe the use of alternative financing channels (as in the Netherland Antilles case) to avoid tax. However, unless the tax covers all financial assets, lender-side substitution is inevitable.

C. Divining the Overall Effects in a Complicated Environment

The different "complications" considered above make it difficult to assess *a priori* the effects of a new withholding tax. Table 2 summarizes the ways these different dimensions of the economic environment influence the welfare analysis. As the table makes clear, some of these complications—namely, U.S. market power and prior taxes on saving—tend to exert positive influences on welfare, offsetting the negative overall impacts implied by the original "simplest case" analysis and the negative influence of prior investment taxes. Thus, in a complex environment, the overall impact of a withholding tax is analytically ambiguous. The overall impact depends on the relative importance of the often contradictory forces at work.

Ascertaining the overall effects requires a quantitative analysis: data and behavioral parameters have to be supplied. The next section discusses the design and results of a quantitative approach intended to shed further light on welfare and other effects of a new withholding tax.

IV. SIMULATIONS

A. The Model

The simulation results described here derive from a simulation model of the U.S. and the "rest of the world." The model is general equilibrium in nature, accounting for interactions among labor, capital, and goods markets in the U.S. and foreign economies. It acknowledges the openness of

TABLE 2
Significance of "Complicating Factors"

Factor	Significance
U.S. Power in Financial Markets	
—large share of world transactions	enables withholding tax (WHT) to cause reduction in domestic and foreign interest rates; makes WHT more (less) attractive if U.S. is net importer (exporter) of capital.
—imperfect substitutability between domestic and foreign securities	enables WHT to induce reduction in domestic interest rate relative to foreign rate; makes WHT more attractive
Tax Credits Offered by Foreign Governments	
—marginal investor fully eligible for credit	enable WHT to transfer funds from foreign to domestic treasuries; imply WHT has no first-order effect on domestic saving or investment
—marginal investor not fully eligible for credit	enable WHT to transfer funds from foreign to domestic treasuries; imply WHT has some effect on domestic saving and investment
Pre-existing Taxes on Domestic Saving or Investment	prior saving taxes expand potential of WHT to generate welfare gains; prior investment taxes reduce this potential
Substitution between Taxed and Untaxed U.S. Securities	implies lower effective withholding tax rate

the U.S. economy by paying close attention to U.S. international trade in commodities and in financial capital.

The model's structure and data are fully described in Goulder and Eichengreen (1989b). Here we offer only a brief description of the model, emphasizing the features most relevant to analyzing withholding taxes.

The production side of the model distinguishes ten U.S. industries and one foreign industry. At each point in time, domestic and foreign producers combine cost-minimizing levels of labor and intermediate inputs with the existing capital stock. Intermediate inputs can be obtained both at home and abroad, and firms choose the mix of domestic and foreign inputs that minimizes costs.

Industry capital stocks evolve over time as a result of managers' forward-looking investment strategies aimed at maximizing the value of the firm. Optimal investment involves balancing the costs of new capital (both the acquisition costs and the adjustment costs associated with installation) against the benefits in terms of the higher gross profits made possible by a larger capital stock.[27] Investments are financed through retained earnings and new issues of debt and equity. Managers have perfect-foresight expectations; thus their investment decisions take account of future prices and interest rates as well as current conditions.

The consumption side of the model includes a representative domestic household and a representative foreign household. Each household makes consumption and portfolio decisions to maximize utility. Like producers, households are forward-looking (with perfect foresight), basing their decisions on future as well as current prices and interest rates. The model takes account of international cross-ownership of financial assets. Portfolios of foreign households, for example, generally consist of both foreign and U.S. stocks and bonds. Similarly for U.S. households.

Households' portfolio decisions include choosing the shares of domestic and foreign assets in their financial wealth. When relative rates of return offered on domestic and foreign assets change, households adjust their portfolios to increase the share of portfolios represented by assets whose relative returns have increased. For a given household, overall consumption at each point in time is a composite of specific consumption good types which in turn are composites of domestically-produced and foreign-made goods of each type. When the relative prices of domestic and foreign consumer goods change, households alter the proportions of domestic and foreign consumer goods making up each composite in accordance with utility maximization.

Household labor supply is exogenous. Households supply labor only to firms in the country of residence: labor is internationally immobile. However, labor is perfectly mobile across industries within a country.

The model also incorporates a government sector in both the domestic and foreign economies. Each government collects taxes, distributes transfers, purchases goods and services, and faces a budget constraint according to which revenues and expenditures must balance in each year.

The requirements of equilibrium are that in each country and in each period of time: (1) the demand for labor equals its supply, (2) the demand for output from each industry equals its supply, (3) total external borrowing by firms equal total saving by residents of the given country

---

[27] The model adopts the asset price approach to investment of Summers (1981), which incorporates considerations of adjustment costs within a q-theoretic firm-value-maximizing investment framework.

plus the net capital inflow, and (4) government revenues equal government spending. Equilibrium is established through adjustments in the nominal exchange rate,[28] in domestic and foreign output prices, in domestic and foreign interest rates, and in lump-sum adjustments to domestic and foreign personal taxes.

New policies lead to changes in prices, interest rates, and asset values in the U.S. and abroad. Such changes induce households to alter their expenditure patterns and their portfolios. Through adjustments in asset prices, interest rates, and exchange rates, a new equilibrium is established in which asset, commodity, and factor supplies and demands are in balance.

B. The Experiments

We consider two main policy changes. The first is the unilateral introduction by the U.S. of a 30 percent withholding tax on foreigners' portfolio interest; the second is the introduction of such a tax accompanied by a similar 30 percent tax adopted by foreign governments. The previous section indicated several factors which condition the effects of a withholding tax. These factors are addressed in the following "central case" assumptions (which are altered in subsequent sensitivity analysis):

1. U.S. Power in Financial Markets.   This depends on the U.S. share of world financial capital and the substitutability of U.S. and foreign assets. The simulations assume that the U.S. initially (prior to the policy change) issues 30 percent of securities issued worldwide. The elasticity of substitution between U.S. and foreign assets in portfolios is assumed to be unity.

2. Tax Credits Provided by Foreign Governments.   Marginal investors are assumed to be ineligible for such credits. However, the credits do apply to inframarginal investments (and give rise to international revenue transfers). Credits are assumed to apply to 60 percent of the value of taxes withheld.

3. Pre-existing Taxes.   The model incorporates detailed aspects of the U.S. tax system. The "foreign tax system" has the same structure as that in the U.S., although its tax rates generally differ from the U.S. counterparts.

---

[28] The number of equilibrating "prices" is one less than the number of equilibrium conditions, as one of the equilibrium conditions is redundant from Walras's Law. Both domestic and foreign nominal wages are fixed in their respective currencies. The exchange rate variable permits the relative prices of domestic and foreign labor to vary.

4. Substitutions between Taxed and Untaxed U.S. Securities. The model's capabilities for evaluating withholding taxes are weakest with respect to this issue. Although it represents corporate stocks and bonds explicitly, the model does not explicitly deal with bank deposits or financial intermediation. Thus it cannot explicitly capture substitutions between such deposits and other assets. Nor does the model directly consider borrower-side tax avoidance through establishment of subsidiaries in tax-haven countries. These issues are addressed primitively and indirectly through the assumption that the effective withholding tax rate is 75 percent of the statutory rate.

C. Results

1. Unilateral Withholding Tax. Table 3 displays some principal macroeconomic effects from these simulations. We begin with the effects of a U.S. withholding tax initiative unaccompanied by foreign retaliation.

a. Macroeconomic effects. The U.S. withholding tax tends to generate an increase in U.S. saving (and consumption) and a decline in foreign saving (and consumption). This partly reflects the fact that the policy change raises permanent income of domestic residents and reduces the permanent income of foreigners (discussed in b below). At the same time, the policy change induces foreigners to devote larger shares of their portfolios to foreign, rather than U.S., assets. Thus, changes in both the levels and composition of saving imply a deterioration of the U.S. capital account balance. In the base (or *status quo*) case, the capital account balance is zero. The policy change implies capital account deficits.

The reduction in foreign demand for U.S. assets has two direct consequences. First, it promotes increases in the U.S. before-tax interest rate. This is shown in Figure 2a, which compares the paths of this interest rate under the policy change with its (constant) path in the base case. The second direct effect is a reduction in the exchange rate value of the dollar; this leads to a parallel reduction in the real exchange rate (price index of domestic goods divided by the price index of foreign goods).

The capital account deficit must be financed by a surplus on the current account, whose components are the trade balance and the net interest receipts from abroad. The policy change reduces the value of interest paid to foreigners; net interest receipts are positive immediately following the policy change. However, in the short run, the improvement in this component of the current account is not sufficient to finance the capital account deficit; hence the U.S. must run a trade surplus. However, as the U.S. continues to run capital account deficits, net interest

TABLE 3
Aggregate Effects of Withholding Taxes[1]

Year	U.S. tax alone				U.S. and foreign taxes combined			
	1	4	15	INF	1	4	15	INF
Nominal exch. rate	-0.340	-0.063	0.341	0.499	-0.009	-0.008	-0.015	-0.028
Real exch. rate	-0.307	-0.005	0.369	0.385	-0.008	-0.002	0.006	0.017
Commodity terms of trade[2]	-0.268	-0.001	0.340	0.385	-0.007	-0.002	0.004	0.003
Domestic pre-tax interest rate	7.766	7.683	7.578	7.560	7.583	7.583	7.584	7.584
Wealth[3]								
Domestic non-human wealth	-0.310	0.039	0.605	0.841	-0.069	-0.078	-0.116	-0.179
WK_DD	-0.354	0.168	0.619	0.833	-0.073	0.410	0.372	0.308
WK_DF	0.143	-1.270	0.463	0.922	-0.033	-5.013	-5.046	-5.107
Domestic human wealth	-0.426	-0.239	0.100	0.369	0.093	0.083	0.046	-0.035
Domestic total wealth	-0.407	-0.201	0.166	0.429	0.071	0.061	0.025	-0.054
Foreign non-human wealth	0.465	-0.018	-0.647	-0.717	-0.025	-0.039	-0.067	-0.122
WK_FF	0.485	0.143	-0.449	-0.512	-0.024	0.162	0.134	0.079
WK_FD	-0.015	-4.019	-5.585	-5.838	-0.063	-5.067	-5.094	-5.142
Foreign human wealth	0.200	0.102	-0.051	-0.147	0.043	0.036	0.021	-0.007
Foreign total wealth	0.218	0.085	-0.078	-0.174	0.032	0.026	0.011	-0.017
Real investment								
Domestic	-0.379	-0.231	0.036	0.240	-0.077	-0.089	-0.129	-0.203
Foreign	0.127	0.078	-0.013	-0.101	-0.028	-0.035	-0.053	-0.087

Real consumption							
Domestic	-0.114	0.016	0.248	0.427	0.023	0.017	-0.005	-0.053
Foreign	0.058	-0.006	-0.108	-0.174	0.013	0.010	0.000	-0.016
Real personal saving							
Domestic	4.201	2.822	1.120	0.854	-0.163	-0.179	-0.223	-0.272
Foreign	-1.757	-1.189	-0.599	-0.383	-0.151	-0.136	-0.121	-0.105
Balance of payments							
Trade balance	0.149	0.008	-0.126	-0.219	0.005	0.002	0.001	0.003
Net income flow	0.138	0.157	0.167	0.252	-0.001	-0.001	-0.001	-0.002
Capital account	-0.288	-0.165	-0.041	-0.033	-0.004	-0.001	0.000	0.000
Net foreign asset position	0.037	0.594	0.996	1.572	0.007	0.012	0.008	0.008
Welfare[4]							
Domestic households	0.259					-0.021		
Foreign households	-0.110					-0.005		
Global welfare	-0.003					-0.010		

[1] All figures are percentage changes from the base case path, except for those corresponding to interest rates, which are in percentage points, and to balance of payments accounts, which are expressed as a fraction of base case GDP for the corresponding year. In the base case, the domestic interest is 7.56 percent in each period, and all balance of payments components are zero.

[2] This is defined as the ratio of the domestic producer price index to the foreign producer price index.

[3] WK_ij denotes the value of non-human wealth owned by residents of country i and located in country j. "D" denotes domestic; "F" foreign.

[4] Welfare is defined as the dynamic equivalent variation as a percentage of base case wealth. Global welfare is the sum of domestic and foreign dynamic equivalent variations as a percentage of total domestic and foreign base case wealth.

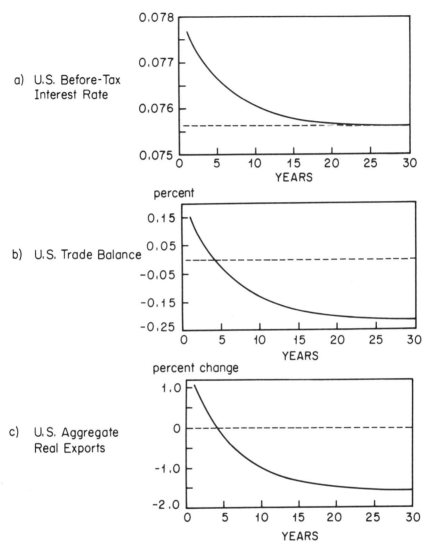

FIGURE 2. *Dynamic Effects of Withholding Taxes*

flows from abroad continue to rise both absolutely and relative to GDP. After a few years, this permits the U.S. trade balance to switch to a deficit, as indicated in Figure 2b. Thus the effects of the withholding initiative on the trade balance change dramatically over time.

On impact, the policy change improves the net foreign asset position of the U.S.—the value of U.S.-owned assets located abroad relative to foreign-owned assets located in the U.S. This occurs because the with-holding tax significantly reduces the after-tax value of foreigners' hold-ings of U.S. assets. The improvement in the U.S. asset position also means that the nation needs to export less to meet its obligations to foreigners.[29]

By raising U.S. pre-tax rates relative to foreign rates, the policy change reduces the rate of domestic investment relative to foreign investment. Over time, this reduces the relative supply of U.S. goods, and tends to raise their relative price, as indicated by the gradual increase in the real exchange rate (after its initial drop). These exchange rate movements help to bring about the necessary changes in the trade balance. They also imply reductions (relative to the base case path) in aggregate real exports in the long run (Figure 2c).

b. Welfare effects. The bottom rows of Table 3 display welfare effects. The policy initiative raises aggregate domestic welfare; this suggests that the positive welfare effects associated with market power and (in the presence of prior saving taxes) increased domestic saving are strong enough to offset the distortionary costs of the policy. Foreigners suffer a decline in welfare. Global welfare—here defined as the sum of the dollar-equivalent welfare changes to domestic and foreign residents—also declines, suggesting that the policy change reduces the global efficiency of resource allocation. (Section V below offers explanations for the global efficiency effects.)

2. U.S. Tax with Foreign Retaliation. The right-hand columns of Table 3 display results under the assumption that the U.S. policy move induces foreigners to respond in kind. The effects in this case are quite different. The symmetric aspect of the two policies implies much smaller changes in the trade balance and other components of the balance of payments. Accordingly, the changes in nominal and real exchange rates are small. While net flows show little change, *gross* international flows change substantially. Because the changes in gross flows largely offset each other, there is relatively little change in available funds to U.S. firms, and before-tax U.S. interest rates change very little.

Global imposition of withholding leads to significant changes in wel-fare. As indicated in Table 3, aggregate domestic as well as foreign welfare decline. A comparison of the results in the two alternative exper-

---

[29] A nation's current account is the change in its net foreign asset position. This relation-ship implies that the present value of a nation's prospective trade balances must equal the negative of its current net foreign asset position. Thus, when the net foreign asset position improves, the trade balance can be lower on average.

iments makes clear that from the point of domestic welfare, the attractiveness of the withholding tax option depends fundamentally on the extent to which it induces foreign retaliation.

3. Sensitivity Analysis. Table 4 shows the sensitivity of results to changes in key parameters. As predicted, lower asset substitutability increases U.S. financial market power, enabling U.S. capital markets to clear with smaller increases in before-tax interest rates. Greater U.S. market power implies lower foreign welfare. The extent of (inframarginal) tax credits to foreigners has relatively little influence on U.S. inter-

TABLE 4
Sensitivity Analysis

	Domestic before-tax interest rate		Trade balance		Welfare		
	SR	LR	SR	LR	Domestic	Foreign	Global
1. Central case	7.766	7.560	0.149	−0.219	0.259	−0.110	−0.010
2. International asset substitutability							
low	7.703	7.560	0.048	−0.189	0.268	−0.117	−0.013
high	7.961	7.560	0.599	−0.422	0.257	−0.108	−0.009
3. Tax credits offered by foreign governments							
restricted	7.777	7.560	0.173	−0.224	0.263	−0.115	−0.013
extended	7.763	7.561	0.156	−0.214	0.258	−0.105	−0.007
marginal investor eligible	7.655	7.561	0.006	−0.180	0.258	−0.107	−0.008
4. No prior taxes on domestic saving and investment	5.695	5.587	0.114	−0.162	0.174	−0.072	−0.006
5. Statutory withholding rate							
15 percent	7.665	7.561	0.083	−0.113	0.133	−0.056	−0.005
60 percent	7.991	7.559	0.326	−0.413	0.499	−0.214	−0.021

"SR" and "LR" denote the first period following the policy change and the new steady state. The status quo or base case value for the domestic interest rate is 7.56 percent, except in the "no-prior-taxes" experiment, for which the base case interest rate is 5.587 percent. In the central case, the elasticity of substitution between domestic and foreign assets in the foreigner's portfolio preference function is unity, the foreign government offers tax credits to foreigners for 60 percent of the value of withholding taxes paid to the U.S., the marginal foreign investor is assumed to be ineligible for tax credits, and the statutory withholding tax rate is 30 percent. The low and high asset substitutability cases assume values of 0.5 and 4.0 for the asset substitution parameter. In the restricted and extended tax credit cases, 30 percent and 90 percent of the value of withholding taxes paid are eligible for tax credits. In the case where the marginal foreign investor is eligible for credits, still only 60 percent of (inframarginal) withholding taxes paid are offset by foreign tax credits.

est rates. Foreign residents' welfare improves slightly with more extensive credits.[30] Treating the marginal foreign investor as eligible for the credits leads to significantly different initial interest rate effects, as expected: the U.S. interest rate need not rise much, since under these circumstances the withholding tax has no first-order effect on the after-tax return to the foreign investor. Here the withholding tax does little to deter foreign investment in the U.S.; hence no serious capital account deficit arises, and the nation can afford to run a trade deficit, even in the short term.[31] A simulation performed under the counterfactual specification of no prior taxes on domestic saving and investment leads to smaller welfare gains from withholding. This suggests that, in the presence of saving and investment taxes, the gains from withholding-tax-induced increases in domestic saving outweigh the losses from induced reductions in domestic investment. Finally, the pattern of interest rate, trade balance, and welfare effects is essentially the same under different statutory withholding rates, although magnitudes differ.

The sensitivity analysis shows that two main results from these experiments are robust. In all experiments, the policy change ultimately worsens the trade balance. In addition, the unilateral initiative considered here consistently leads to domestic welfare gains. Still, these results should be interpreted with caution. Results are sensitive to assumptions about the extent of asset substitutability, and very high values could reverse the sign of the welfare effect.[32] In addition, the lack of an explicit treatment of banking institutions and other financial intermediation is a significant limitation in evaluating this withholding initiative. It should also be kept in mind that all simulations assume balanced budgets on the part of the U.S. and foreign governments: revenue-expenditure balance is maintained through lump-sum tax adjustments. Hence these experiments do not account for possible welfare effects associated with the withholding tax's ability to alter public sector budget imbalances (the U.S. budget deficit in particular). These results should be regarded as suggestive rather than definitive.

---

[30] One might expect higher credits to imply lower foreign welfare. In the model, the potentially adverse effects of higher credits are minimized because the credits are financed through lump-sum taxes, which have no direct adverse efficiency consequences.

[31] The trade balance is slightly positive in year 1 but is negative in all subsequent years.

[32] For technical reasons, we were unable to employ values larger than 4.0 for the asset substitutability parameter. Employing very large values currently leads to instability in the algorithm used to solve for economic equilibria. One hopes that a technical breakthrough is not far away.

V. ADOPTING A MORE GLOBAL PERSPECTIVE

The approach taken in the last two sections to evaluate the withholding tax option might be considered narrow in at least two respects. First, it employed a somewhat restrictive notion of U.S. welfare. Considerations of international fairness, of the good (or bad) will stemming from perceptions of fairness (or inequity), and of the global efficiency of resource allocation were omitted from the previous assessments of the tax.

Second, the previous sections evaluated the policy option only in comparison with the *status quo*, whereas a broader examination might expand the domain of alternatives to include coordinated policy initiatives undertaken cooperatively by the U.S. and other nations. Such initiatives might lead to more favorable outcomes (domestically and globally) than the non-cooperative policy actions scrutinized thus far. This section takes a broader perspective, investigating some issues that may be critical to the overall attractiveness of the withholding tax option.

A. A Beggar-Thy-Neighbor Policy or a Quid-Pro-Quo Response?

The simulation results from the previous section indicate that a unilateral withholding tax would generate welfare losses to foreigners that largely offset the domestic welfare gains. It is hard to justify unilateral introduction of the tax on the grounds of global efficiency, since the reductions in foreign wealth and welfare match the domestic gains. The unilateral policy has an unappealing beggar-thy-neighbor quality.

The initiative gains some appeal to the extent that it is applied selectively, only to residents *of those countries that already impose similar levies on the interest income of U.S. residents.* A selective withholding tax seems less unfair. Table 5 shows the withholding taxes that 25 (mainly industrialized) countries apply to income earned from U.S. portfolio investments in those countries. The table reveals considerable variation in the treatment of interest income. Three of the nations offer a blanket exemption for interest income. Nine others exempt such income as a result of treaties with the U.S. Twelve countries tax interest income at rates of ten percent or higher. The table suggests that if a U.S. tax on foreigners' portfolio interest were imposed selectively, it might apply to about half of the major nations involved in international financial transactions with the U.S.

B. Global Efficiency

However, whether or not it is imposed selectively, a withholding tax on interest income is not attractive in terms of the global efficiency of capital

TABLE 5
Foreign Withholding Rates on U.S.-Owned Capital Under U.S. Income Tax Treaties (as of January 1, 1988)

Country	Dividends %	Interest %	Patent and Know-How Royalties %
Australia	15	10	10
Austria	10	E	E
Belgium	15	15	E
Canada	15	15	10
China	10	10	10
Cyprus	0	10	0
Denmark	15	E	E
Egypt	N/A	15	15
Finland	15	0	0
France	15	0	5
Germany (West)	15	E	E
Greece	N/A	E	E
Ireland	N/A	E	E
Italy	15	15	10
Japan	15	10	10
Korea (South)	15	12	15
Luxembourg	7.5	E	E
Netherlands	15	E	E
New Zealand	15	10	10
Norway	15	0	E
Philippines	25	15	25
Sweden	15	E	E
Switzerland	15	5	E
Trinidad & Tobago	25	15	15
United Kingdom	15	E	E

Definitions:
E, The income is exempt from withholding tax under the treaty. N/A, The treaty does not limit the tax applicable to this type of income.

Note: Rates apply to both individual and corporate investors. Source of data is Ernst & Whinney, *1988 Foreign and U.S. Corporate Income and Withholding Tax Rates.*

allocation. The policy experiments described in the previous section attest to this result: for example, simulations of a unilateral expansion of the U.S. withholding tax led to no increase in global welfare. A reason for the global inefficiency of the withholding tax is that it departs from the *residence principle* of taxation, which has some desirable efficiency properties. When taxed on a residence basis, households pay taxes on their worldwide income, and their tax obligations are to the governments of their country of residence. Universal adoption of the residence principle in the taxation of capital income tends to promote a more efficient global allocation of capital by inducing equality of pre-tax rates of return on capital, even when nations' tax rates differ.[33]

The withholding tax does not adhere to the residence principle. The tax is *source-based:* an individual's withholding tax obligations are to the country in which the income is generated, not the country of residence. When nations impose different tax rates, source-based taxation cannot be relied upon to produce a globally efficient allocation of capital: pre-tax returns will generally not be equated. Introducing withholding taxes leads tax systems away from the residence principle and is likely to imply a reduction in the global efficiency of capital allocation. This adverse effect is mitigated to the extent that foreign governments allow their residents to credit withholding taxes paid to the U.S.[34]

A second major reason for the global efficiency losses has to do with the changes in the overall level of capital taxation brought about by expanding the withholding tax. While the previous discussion of residence-based taxation was linked to the efficiency in the *static international* allocation of capital, the issue of the overall level of capital taxation bears on the efficiency in the *intertemporal* allocation of capital. Insofar as they raise the overall level of capital taxation, expanded withholding taxes may reduce the intertemporal efficiency of resource allocation, leading to lower levels of saving and investment than that which would maximize welfare over time.[35] In the simulations reported in the previous section, the expanded withholding tax did indeed augment the overall level of capital taxation because the additional taxes were not

---

[33] See Bovenberg (1989b), Giovannini (1989), and Mintz (1986) for a discussion of the efficiency of residence-based (and source-based) taxation. Although universal adoption of residence-based taxation may yield a "neutral" tax environment in the sense that pre-tax rates of return are equal across countries and industries, if consumption-side taxes are not optimal or if different types of capital goods are not equally complementary to labor in production, neutrality of this type is generally sub-optimal. On this point see Auerbach (1988). Furthermore, multinational firms introduce complications, and residence-based taxation of such firms cannot guarantee production efficiency (see Mintz [1986]).

It may be noted that the OECD, in its 1977 Model Double Taxation Convention on Income and on Capital, endorsed the residence principle for interest income flows as a rule for double taxation treaties.

[34] When foreign governments allow their residents to credit 100 percent of withholding taxes paid to the U.S., the marginal tax rate faced by foreigners on investments in the U.S. is that of the home (foreign) country. In this case the efficiency properties of residence-based taxation are retailed.

[35] If agents effectively face infinite horizons, capital allocation is intertemporally efficient in the absence of taxes. Capital income taxes may lead to a path of consumption that is sub-optimal in terms of intertemporally defined utility: there will be too much present consumption (too little saving) and too little future consumption. See Sandmo (1976).

offset by reductions in other capital taxes.[36] Thus, the policy initiative is likely to have led to a reduction in the efficiency in the intertemporal as well as the international allocation of capital.[36a]

C. Are Efficiency and Fairness Goals Reconcilable?

These considerations suggest a conflict between efficiency and equity goals. While it may seem fair for the U.S. to impose additional withholding taxes selectively on residents of countries which impose similar taxes, doing so may well worsen the global efficiency of resource allocation. The outcome does not appear to be fully satisfactory. Are there other worthwhile options?

One alternative worth considering involves international tax coordination. A principal goal of such coordination would be achieving a wider international application of the residence principle. One means to this end would be removal of withholding taxes by those nations that currently impose them. To the extent that other nations agree to such measures, there is less justification on equity grounds for an expanded U.S. tax. However, until multilateral reductions in withholding taxes are agreed to, the temporary introduction of U.S. withholding on portfolio interest might have some value as a bargaining chip. But such U.S. withholding would not be intended as a permanent fixture.

Unfortunately, in the context of the withholding tax, international policy coordination faces serious political obstacles. Nations removing existing withholding taxes face the dilemma of reduced tax revenues or of having to increase other taxes. The prevalence of withholding taxes may stem from the fact that they involve relatively small political costs: those who must pay these taxes have a relatively small political voice within the country in question. Replacing withholding taxes with taxes on domestic residents, on the other hand, may involve very large political costs. Thus the political barriers to greater adoption of residence-based taxation through the removal of withholding taxes are formidable.

---

[36] The policy simulations involved lump-sum reductions in individual labor and capital income taxes. These adjustments were made at the level necessary to assure that in each policy experiment, total tax revenues to each country were the same as those collected in each country in the base (*status quo*) case. Because these adjustments were lump-sum and not restricted to capital, the simulations implied an increase in overall (inclusive of the withholding tax) capital taxation.

[36a] Higher capital taxes may permit given levels of government expenditure to be provided with lower taxes on labor. The efficiency losses attributable to higher capital taxes can conceivably be offset by efficiency gains from lower labor taxes. The model employed in this paper does not capture these potential offsetting effects, since household labor supply is exogenous.

D. Tax Evasion and Capital Flight

Several analysts have pointed out that a significant amount of foreign investment in the U.S. is undertaken in order to evade taxation in the country of residence.[37] Many nations that officially adopt the residence principle have difficulty preventing tax evasion because of limited information concerning income earned from abroad: if investments made outside the country of residence are not monitored, then such investments can provide a vehicle for escaping taxes. This problem is particularly severe for less developed countries (LDCs). The cost is not simply a loss of tax revenues but also a lower rate of domestic capital accumulation and growth.

These difficulties reverse the usual fairness arguments about withholding. Referring to the tax evasion problem, some analysts contend that fairness considerations argue *for* the expansion of a U.S. withholding tax. If the U.S. withholds foreigners' interest income, it is no longer possible to escape capital income taxation by investing in the U.S. Thus, U.S. withholding of portfolio interest has the virtue of discouraging tax evasion and capital flight.

The problems of tax evasion and capital flight are indeed serious. However, introducing a U.S. withholding tax on portfolio interest may not be the most effective remedy for these difficulties. The evasion problem ultimately stems from a lack of information on foreign investments; the most natural solution may be to develop better ways to monitor investments in the U.S. and provide information on these investments to foreign governments. Certainly providing information would not eliminate all tax evasion, capital flight to the U.S., or capital flight to other countries. But such efforts would appear to be at least as effective in addressing these problems as an expanded U.S. withholding tax. At the same time, it would avoid many of the inefficiencies that enlarging the U.S. withholding tax would generate.

However, any unilateral efforts undertaken by the U.S. are likely to be limited in their effectiveness in dealing with tax evasion problems. So long as other nations continue to offer favorable investment opportunities, unilateral provision of information or expansion of the U.S. withholding tax would have the effect of inducing investors from LDCs to redirect their investments from the U.S. to other nations. Only through cooperative efforts on the part of all "tax haven" countries can these problems be addressed effectively.[38]

---

[37] See, for example, Bird and McLure (1988) and McLure (1989).

[38] See McLure (1989) for a detailed discussion of this issue.

VI. CONCLUSIONS

The complexities of international financial markets and of international politics make evaluating the withholding tax option a difficult matter. Existing treaty provisions as well as tax-avoidance options on both the supply and demand sides of securities markets substantially limit the opportunities to obtain additional revenues through expansion of the U.S. withholding tax.

The introduction of a statutory 30 percent U.S. withholding tax on foreigners' interest income, if not accompanied by similar (retaliatory) tax measures by foreign governments, appears to yield aggregate domestic welfare gains. The gains are attributable to U.S. financial market power and to induced increases in domestic saving. U.S. market power stems from the large share represented by the U.S. of world financial transactions and from the imperfect substitutability between U.S. and foreign securities in portfolios. Simulations suggest that these gains more than compensate for adverse distortionary effects of the tax. Although the tax initially has a favorable effect on the U.S. trade balance and aggregate exports, it ultimately has the opposite effect. The common proposition that a withholding tax would help relieve the U.S. trade deficit appears to be valid only for the short term.

On the other hand, if foreign governments respond in kind to the U.S. introduction of withholding on portfolio interest, U.S. residents' aggregate welfare declines. Under these circumstances, effects on net trade flows and on the U.S. net foreign asset position are much smaller.

Regardless of whether it is matched by similar measures by foreign governments, expanding the U.S. withholding tax seems to imply a reduction in the global efficiency of resource allocation. The efficiency costs may arise because the tax represents a departure from the residence principle of taxation (to the extent that foreign governments do not provide credits for U.S. withholding taxes paid) and because it implies an increase in the overall level of capital taxation.

The equity arguments for the withholding tax are mixed. An unappealing feature of a unilateral U.S. withholding tax initiative is that the gains in U.S. welfare come at the expense of foreigners. Restricting the application of the tax to investors from countries that already impose similar measures may have more justification on fairness grounds than applying the tax to all foreign investors. An attraction of the tax is its ability to discourage capital flight to the U.S. and associated tax evasion; however, other policies with less serious efficiency costs might be equally effective in addressing tax evasion problems.

APPENDIX

1. Welfare Implications of Financial Market Power of U.S.

Define r_m as the return paid to foreigners on K_m, U.S. capital imports; r_m is therefore the U.S. interest rate net of the withholding tax. Define r_x as the return paid to U.S. residents on K_x, U.S. capital exports (U.S. residents' portfolio investments abroad); if foreigners do not impose withholding taxes, this is simply the gross rate of return offered abroad translated into dollars. By calculating the foreign rate in dollar terms, one avoids the need to consider exchange rate movements explicitly.

A large share of world financial transactions and imperfect substitutability between domestic and foreign securities can (each) alter the welfare effects of a withholding tax through their influence on $r_x K_x - r_m K_m$, the value of net interest income to the U.S. Large market share enables a U.S. withholding tax to drive down the rates r_m and r_x. If securities are perfect substitutes, then r_m must equal r_x. The welfare influence depends on the induced change in $r_x K_x - r_m K_m$, and since $r_x = r_m$, it depends on the change in $r(K_x - K_m)$, where r represents the common international interest rate. If the U.S. is a net capital exporter ($K_x > K_m$) and the tax doesn't alter much the difference between K_x and K_m, then the induced reduction in r lowers net interest income and thereby has a negative influence on welfare. The reverse is the case for a net capital importer.

Imperfect asset substitutability enables the U.S. to force down r_m below the rate r_x. This is possible even when the U.S. share of world financial transactions is small. Again, the influence on welfare depends on the induced change in $r_x K_x - r_m K_m$. Ceteris paribus, lower asset substitutability allows for a larger relative reduction in r_m. This implies an increase in domestic net interest income. Thus, lower asset substitutability tends to exert a positive influence on the domestic welfare effects of withholding.

2. Welfare Implications of Prior Taxes on Domestic Saving and Investment

a. Prior Taxes on Saving.   Figure 3a indicates the economic equilibria that result in the presence and absence of pre-existing taxes on domestic saving. The OCS and MPC schedules represent the opportunity cost of saving and marginal product of capital, as before. In the absence of taxes, these schedules correspond to supply curves for domestic saving and investment. For an economy that is a price-taker in capital markets, equilibrium domestic saving and investment are at levels S_{D1} and I_{D1}. Introducing a withholding tax at the rate t_w yields equilibrium saving

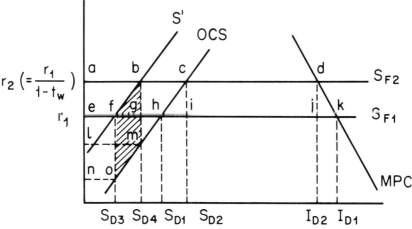

FIGURE 3a. *Effects of Withholding Tax in Presence of Prior Saving Taxes*

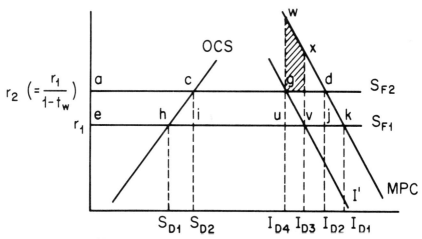

FIGURE 3b. *Effects of Withholding Tax in Presence of Prior Investment Taxes*

and investment of S_{D2} and I_{D2}. The aggregate welfare loss is given by the triangular regions *cih* and *dkj*, corresponding to the regions B and D described previously in Section III.

The implications of a prior tax on domestic saving are as follows. The domestic supply curve is now S', where the horizontal distance between S' and *OCS* is the tax paid per unit of saving. In the absence of withholding, equilibrium domestic saving is now S_{d3}, while equilibrium domestic investment is still I_{D1}. Introducing a withholding tax in this environment leads to a new equilibrium with domestic saving and investment of S_{D4} and I_{D2}, respectively. Under these conditions, domestic savers gain the region *lmon*, which, if saving taxes are proportional, corresponds to the region *abfe*. Domestic borrowers, as before, lose *adke*. Taxpayers gain the withholding tax revenues *cdji* + *fbmo* (shaded region), the taxes collected on the additional saving $S_{D4} - S_{D3}$. The aggregate welfare loss is *bfg* + *dkj* less the additional saving taxes, *fbmo*. Under proportional saving taxes, *bgf* corresponds to *cih*; thus, the difference between the aggregate welfare effect in this case and in the case without prior saving taxes is *fbmo*. This area is the gain associated with realizing the excess of the marginal social benefit of saving over its marginal social cost as domestic saving rises from S_{D3} to S_{D4}.

A similar analysis can be employed to show that prior progressive saving taxes do not augment the potential gains (or reduce the losses) from a withholding tax as much as prior proportional saving taxes do: the improvement in welfare relative to the case of no prior saving taxes will be less than the value of the induced new saving taxes.

b. Prior Taxes on Investment.   The analysis for prior investment taxes is analogous. Figure 3b indicates the economic equilibria in the presence and absence of such prior taxes. If there are no prior taxes, equilibrium saving and investment are S_{D1} and I_{D1} with no withholding and S_{D2} and I_{D2} following the imposition of a withholding tax.

With a tax on investment, the investment schedule is I' and equilibrium domestic saving and investment are S_{D1} and I_{D3} before withholding. Implementing the withholding tax leads to the equilibrium with saving and investment of S_{D2} and I_{D4}. Domestic savers gain *ache* and domestic borrowers lose *aqve*. Taxpayers gain *cqui* in withholding tax revenues *but lose* the revenues *wxvq* (shaded region) that previously were collected from the investment tax. The aggregate loss is *cih* + *qvu* plus *wxvq*, the lost investment tax revenues. Under proportional investment taxes, *qvu* equals *dkj*; hence in these circumstances pre-existing investment taxes imply that aggregate welfare losses will be larger by the amount of foregone investment tax revenue, *wxvq*. This area is the

loss associated with the failure to enjoy the excess of the marginal social benefit of investment over its marginal social cost for potential investments from I_{D4} to I_{D3}. A similar analysis reveals that under progressive investment taxes, the aggregate welfare losses exceed the losses with no prior investment taxes by an amount less than the value of foregone investment tax revenue.

REFERENCES

Auerbach, A. J. 1988. The deadweight loss from "non-neutral" capital income taxation. National Bureau of Economic Research working paper no. 2510. February.

Bird, R. M. and C. E. McLure, Jr. 1989. The personal income tax in an interdependent world. Mimeo.

Bovenberg, A. L. 1989a. The effects of capital income taxation on international competitiveness and trade flows. *American Economic Review 79* (forthcoming).

———. 1989b. International coordination of tax policies. International Monetary Fund. Mimeo.

Bovenberg, A. L. and L. H. Goulder. 1989. Promoting investment under international capital mobility: An intertemporal general equilibrium analysis. National Bureau of Economic Research working paper no. 3139. October.

Brean, D. J. S. 1984. *International issues in taxation: The Canadian perspective.* Canadian tax paper no. 75. Canadian Tax Foundation.

Carson, M. P. 1985. Foreign recipients of U.S. income, and tax withheld, 1984. *SOI Bulletin.* Department of the Treasury, Internal Revenue Service, vol. 5, no. 2. pp. 61–77.

Giovannini, A. 1989. National tax systems vs. the European capital market. *Economic Policy.* October.

Goulder, L. H. and B. Eichengreen. 1989a. Savings promotion, investment promotion and international competitiveness. In *Trade policies for international competitiveness,* R. Feenstra, ed. Chicago: University of Chicago Press.

———. 1989b. Final report for phase II research on a computable general equilibrium model for analyzing dynamic responses to trade policy and foreign competition. Prepared for Bureau of International Labor Affairs of the U.S. Department of Labor.

King, M. A. and D. Fullerton. 1984. *The taxation of income from capital.* Chicago: University of Chicago Press.

Lewis, M. P. 1986. Foreign recipients of U.S. income, and tax withheld. *SOI Bulletin.* Department of the Treasury, Internal Revenue Service, vol. 6, no. 2. pp. 61–77.

McLure, C. E., Jr. 1989. U.S. tax laws and capital flight from Latin America. *Inter-American Law Review* 20 (2), University of Miami.

Mintz, J. M. 1986. Corporate tax design in an international setting: tax competition and the openness of the economy. Kingston, Ontario: Queens University. Mimeo. June.

Papke, L. E. 1988. International differences in capital taxation and corporate borrowing behavior: Evidence from the U.S. withholding tax. Boston: School of Management, Boston University. Mimeo.

Sandmo, A. 1976. Optimal taxation—and introduction to the literature. *Journal of Public Economics* 6. pp. 37–54.

Scholl, R. B. 1984. The international investment position of the U.S. in 1983. *Survey of Current Business.* June. pp. 74–77.

———. 1985. The international investment position of the U.S. in 1984. *Survey of Current Business.* June. pp. 25–33.

———. 1986. The international investment position of the U.S. in 1985. *Survey of Current Business.* June. pp. 26–35.

———. 1988. The international investment position of the U.S. in 1987. *Survey of Current Business.* June. pp. 76–84.

———. 1989. The international investment position of the U.S. in 1988. *Survey of Current Business.* June. pp. 41–49.

Sinn, H. W. 1988. The 1986 U.S. tax reform and the world capital market. *European Economic Review* 32. pp. 325–33.

Summers, L. H. 1981. Taxation and corporate investment: A q-theory approach. *Brookings Papers on Economic Activity.* (January): 67–127.